MEA CULPA

(ADMISSION OF GUILT)

Sarah Machir-Grant

Disclaimer:

For Paul and Rose,
Pratchett once wrote that: 'it's better to light a flamethrower than to curse the darkness.' I was fortunate to have two people standing ready with the match. Thank you.

And for Peter, because with you I am me.

Acknowledgements

Special thanks to Dot for your constant support, encouragement and feedback.

Contents

I

SUB LOVE FRIGIDO

(Beneath Cold Jupiter)

You can spend a lifetime running from the things that you want to forget, but eventually, those memories will catch up with you, and when they do, the distance that you've covered will make no difference to the depth of their ferocity. Those raging recollections will eat you up if you're not careful, and all the diligent work that you put into trying to avoid them will have been for nothing. I guess this was how it was for me anyway, when all the furnishings of the carefully prosaic life that I'd constructed to conceal myself from the gaping jaws of what lays beneath just fell away as dry leaves on the autumn breeze, the lies that I told myself in the darkness of night became like dust beneath my knees, pale, taught and unmoving, as I knelt there rocking behind the door, waiting for the world as I knew it to finally and irreversibly end.

1

MEA CULPA

It is a miracle of the human mind that what might be thought of as long forgotten can suddenly come back with all the clarity and lightning force of something that we experienced only yesterday. All the depth of emotion, all the rigour of reaction. None of the hindsight. And as I cowered behind the door that night, the things that I had walked away from, the things that I had tried so hard to forget, the things that had crushed me once before, well, those things found their way back through. They rematerialised those wispy apparitions of my mind, feeding from the desolation that welled beneath the carefully polished veneer of a well-disciplined existence, and this time there was nowhere left to run.

Outside and beyond, it was a November evening; cold, direct, and dark in every way that an evening should be when our hemisphere of the earth is tilted far away from the life-giving sun. It remains memorable to me now only because of the impending freeze, which would come early and hit hard, leaving a frosting of white everywhere those icy tendrils touched. I always think of it as duplicitous, the snow that forms later in drifts and banks, and as I looked out through the thin pane into the picture window scene that day or the next, it gave a sort of illusion of purity that made the innocent and young of heart reach out with tentative rosy-pink fingers, only to discover the sharp solid ice barely beneath the surface. A coldness that broke backs and limbs.

I always look for some sign of risk or danger, where others can just enjoy the moment. Sometimes, I wonder if it's because I only ever truly exist in one moment, whereas these others have the luxury of so many. One small moment in time is where I remain, huddled in some small space, choking for air and lightheaded from lack of it. Of course, it is not a moment in the strictest sense but has the feeling of being momentary because it has passed into the realms of recollection. Like the flashes on a billboard as the train whirrs quickly by. Present and not present. And not one singular event in the strictest sense but rather the feeling of something that has happened in some simultaneous manner when recalled from the realms of a murky reminiscence. It is a moment of many moments that exists beyond November, beyond winter roads and icy paths. It is a moment undefined by the confines of temporal language or chronological order. A moment that has extended beyond all moments, beyond time, beyond worlds, beyond reckoning. Within that moment, that single moment of experience, right there, right then, all that exists in that moment is fear. And me. I also exist in that moment.

They say those who reduce the human experience to its chemical compounds and biological pathways, well, they say that fear is an emotional response. Fear is a natural reaction to a threat, a stimulation of the amygdala, the most primal part of our brain, which produces a rush of adrenaline when we become afraid. A rush of hormones gives us that all-too-familiar fight or flight response. Yes, they say, fear is quite an ordinary process, the transformation of one molecule by another. In fact, they say that this sudden increase of oxygen in the bloodstream, which gives the muscles a quick burst of energy, would have helped our ancestors avoid ancient predators. Fear, then, by all accounts, is designed to give us wings.

But in our cosy westernised, civilised, well-ordered world, fear is not an experience that many of us truly understand because we believe those ancient predators to be tamed; the subject of exhibits, displays, and gruesome late-night television documentaries even. Not alive and hunting us. Hunting us today. So, when real fear comes upon us, there is no biological response, no stimulation of the adrenal glands, and no oxygenation of the bloodstream. When real fear comes knocking, there is no taking off. Somewhere in the evolutionary process, we appear to have lost our wings.

Not me, though. I know fear. I know fear well. Fear is like a greasy old blanket that rests softly on the world, wrapping everything within its reach in the choking smell of its unwashed fibres. Fear clings to your face and your mouth and stops you from screaming into the night. Fear is the thing that prevents you from flying when flight is the only right thing to do. Fear is tangible, actual, and animal. There is absolutely nothing ordinary, natural, or necessary about fear. Once fear comes and rests on you and inside of you, well then, that fear never goes away. There is no remedy, no cure, no type of crystal, no herbal tea, no kind of therapy that will ever eradicate the fear. I have tried them all, and trust me, fear is here to stay.

MEA CULPA

It is all because of this fear, of course, or rather the old familiarity of it, creeping and settling in like a cat that has spent time out in the cold, only to then find the comfort of a warm bed by the fire. It was, it is, there in that place, at that moment that is a place, in that chaotic fraction of time huddled caught in the bindings of fear, motionless, it was here in this place, on that night, that November night beneath cold Jupiter, that the sinking realisation finally sank in.

There was nowhere left to run. I had fled, you see. I had flown. I had used my wings. Oh, and I was diligent. I had reconstructed my world so that every possible aspect remained in some way tangibly changed. But this effort had been in vain because the fear remained. Fear was the only thing that ever truly remained. It would always be just myself and the fear.

So, I huddled alone but for the comfort of fear. Time and space became irrelevant because GMT coordinates, and all these things are trapped relative to somewhere else, sometime else. And there is no place else but here.

I knelt, choking, huddled, and trying hard to breathe through the asphyxiating blanket of fear. I didn't bother to wonder what would happen next. There was no need. After all, fear was the only friend that I could ever fully count on. Fear always delivered as fear promised.

II

EX TEMPORE

(This Moment)

It had been an uneventful sort of day. A day without expectations. A mundane sort of Monday. Another day spent nestled in the cosy protection of drudgery and collective normality.

Mine was a non-descript sort of office job. Much the same as any other non-descript sort of office job. I bobbed about from home to work and back again in the shiny blue four-door hatchback, which was much the same as any other office worker's mode of transport. I wore my light brown hair pinned up and my bright brown eyes pinned forward. Always looking towards tomorrow, always planning ahead. Just like the others. Always the same.

During the day, my refuge would be banks of desks, keyboards, monitors, and the sea of nodding heads that carefully watched the flicker of their LCD screens, glancing surreptitiously upwards at every movement of the circular monochrome wall clock; the collective will of a hundred people only seeming to make the staggered hands tick by more slowly. Finally, the inevitable would arrive, and I, too, would join in their release from the daily grind, hiding in plain sight among the buzzing swarm as they crowded at the exits of the glass-fronted high-rise. Then, just like all the others, I pushed my way through the darting school of flashing vehicles, speeding homewards towards an evening of judiciously prepared and shrewdly narrated social programming and propaganda, politically motivated persuasion marketed as television entertainment packages. Living the dream.

Afterwards, I would follow this up by a good eight hours on some carefully selected 'Drowsitown' mattress, designed for those with bad posture and endorsed by a retired soap opera actress that I had never heard of but on whose authority I was prepared to spend a month's salary.

On waking, it would be a high-fibre breakfast, recommended by an 'industry expert' in my monthly glossy paged fashion subscription. Doing the right thing. Choosing life. My choice of life included a daily seven hours and twenty-four minutes of monitoring and tweaking the fluctuating service performance records at, well, let's just call it Megalamania, where it was important to irrevocably evidence that the customer always came first, while at the same time ensuring above all else, a year on year increase in stakeholders' profits. Tricky business.

Sometimes, I used to sit and ponder over my avocado salad bowl: how did I get from there to here? But the thoughts were short-lived because there was always something new to buy, or do, or make better. There was little time to dwell.

So, on that particular mundane Monday, I had anticipated a regular sort of uneventful routine evening. It was a cold November day that would merge in the memory with other such days like it. I drove home in that bright blue car and ran quickly upstairs through the chill of the beige empty house to peel off the camouflage of my ordinary, uneventful, routine, cold November life because this is what a person did after spending the day studiously working within the banks of sterile office desks and monitors. Lest a speck of dust foul the carefully selected neutral-coloured two-piece uniform of the office worker.

The dark manmade fabrics and crisp cotton blouse identified me as an administrator, taxpayer, and wage earner. Dependable, trustworthy, solid. How peculiar is it that a simple nylon weave might define authority, right, and quality? It is the clothes that maketh the man, and they most certainly maketh the woman. Perhaps this might have been a different kind of story if I had still been wearing those clothes. Should I? Would I? Could I have charged down there concealed in the draping of decency, indignant at the intrusion? Interrupted this encroachment with some affronted outburst. Probably. I knew enough, know enough, about fear to pass fear on. Leave them afraid, not breathing. But as it happens, that high street haute lay discarded on the bedroom floor, and I knelt there huddled in a prudently purchased thin mint bathrobe. Vulnerable and alone. Alone but for the fear. Just like before, and nothing like before.

This moment. That moment. Ordinarily, they pass by unnoticed, those moments of our life, they pass by in anticipation of the next.

When the door burst inwards, I expected to hear a familiar voice, expected the usual routine: dinner, TV, laundry maybe. So much for expectations. Because instead came the quick and sharp realisation that tonight the routine had changed, and not changed. Instead, an old familiarity crept in, slipped in, crawled in, and made itself at home again. I found a convenient door to hide behind because I knew the drill. Fear settled down beside me. Fear also knew the drill. Fear, like a chill and constant companion, a most secret and not-so-imaginary friend.

They pass by unnoticed, those moments, this moment, that moment, but it only takes one to make or break a life.

Later, the blue lights came, flashing bright and blinding. Then sweet tea and furtive glances. Kind words and scripted condolences.

I made, or she made, apologies to the officer. I don't know where the line is anymore. He came to perform the mandatory questioning and issue the customary warnings to ensure that blame was attributed where blame was due. After all, it was almost impossible to catch the perpetrators, while victims of crime were much easier to locate, investigate and castigate. One way or another, the stats must improve.

He issued a crime reference number and a Victim Support Pamphlet: How to Secure Your Property. There was nothing else to do. Forensics are so rarely used outside of American sitcoms; they didn't have the resources to investigate, so what was the point in collecting evidence? Besides, it would be like trying to find a needle in a haystack. I think that's what he said. Public services were stretched enough as they were without adding to the workload. I'd brought it on myself. This bit was implicit. It sat there between us like a stain on the carpet.

He exchanged some words with the husband, with my husband. Man to man—furtive glances my way. Let the little woman rest.

Then, before leaving, a quick: 'Just don't make it so easy for them next time.' Semi-stern and father-like chastisement from the officer. Shame filled my face with scarlet heat. Victim. There was no defence. Guilty as charged, your honour, sorry officer.

MEA CULPA

How could I have been so stupid? Over and over and over again in my head like a loop. Afterwards, I hunched folded into an armchair and looked away to somewhere else, someplace else, sometime else. I can see myself now. They would call it despondent.

In the long moment knelt behind the door with only fear for company, I had glimpsed something long forgotten, yet not forgotten at all. Vast and overpowering, screeching and formidable, towering above, horrendous and intense. They pelted me with insults, spit out their bile, and laughed when I cowered lower, snivelling, begging, pleading, crying out. I hate myself for the snivelling and the begging. Get up, get up, you fucking pussy. But I can't... I can't ever get up. Because I'm swaddled in fear, sobbing, helpless, breathless. Unmoving in a makeshift shroud. I want to get up.

This is the longest of all moments. They laugh, they skip, they chant, they stalk, and they threaten. But I knew better than to tell any kind of officer this. Swathed as I am in my comforting fear, guided by fear's tight embrace, I know only too well what would happen if I started tittering away in some officer's ear. Oh yes, my girl. The fear is drawing closer.

I hug myself now, absent-mindedly seeing the sweet tea still sits cooling on the side. So, it was in the days and weeks to come that the tea would be brought and the tea would cool, and tea would be taken away, while steadily, the carefully crafted world around slowly died and peeled away like brown autumn leaves, landing softly on the ground and rustling underfoot. Bewildered now, I would not lift a finger to either. Instead, metaphorically speaking, I would merely stare around, confounded at a loss and tread lightly here and there on the scattered remnants of my old life, which had once been so attentively planned and nurtured. I was distracted, mostly elsewhere, and had little care in encouraging some green shoot of interest or prospect to grow. I saw no blossoming of the delicate foliage or shooting of the tiny bud-like leaves as the season changed to spring, instead continuing as in ceaseless winter, welcoming only the familiarity of darkness and intimacy of solitude in this strange new land.

Eventually, a sort of numbness took hold and left me motionless and barren, standing still against the cold white sky of my own making, not daring to make a move in case yet more destruction may follow. So, I watched as the next cup of tea grew cold on the side and as everything that I had known slowly crumbled around into dust; my hopes and dreams lifeless grey residue of some former time and the love that I had once felt no longer humming inside the hollow cavity where before a heart had been.

When I could finally no longer stand to see what had been so dear to me become so distant, well then I very delicately, very cautiously, very quietly tiptoed out of the dried, fallen scraps of life, and with purpose and precision, slowly moved away.

Maybe a decision had been made somewhere inside of me to proceed on some bleaker, darker course. It's not like I would have revealed this to anyone, least of all myself. I was both unmoving and afloat. I had an odd sensation of buoyancy about myself, not in the sense of raised spirits but rather the feeling of being almost entirely untethered.

With that, I rented a small house on a small street with small neighbours who were preoccupied enough with their own small lives to pay little attention to one new, relatively small tenant. The tiny yellow brick house had only one door, with good solid locks, and not much garden to speak of, except a small paved area at the back just big enough to hang out some washing. I extricated myself as kindly as could be accomplished in the circumstances from the burdens of responsibility that came with the prosaic life that I had nourished before, like the husband, the home, and societal connections. Instead, I furnished this new existence lightly, not bothering much with decorating the tiny cream interiors. To embellish a home or a life requires some kind of forward-thinking, and right then, the only thing that I saw was my past.

I ate little, read little, worked little, and time ticked by little by little. My resolve changed a little. Although imperceptible at first, even to me, I think that I still clung to some small feeling of hope because I had tasted a form of liberty once before, and maybe I thought that it was possible to sip from this fountain again. Even though this new ashen world was empty, cold and remorseless, drenched in despair, perhaps there was a chance for some small seedling of promise to grow. Whatever the reason might be, each morning, I would rise and dress in that same old, worn-out smile, and no one around would ever notice the tiniest amount of wear.

III

POST EVENTUM

(After the event)

Historians write about great deeds, great wars, and great moments, relating all of this perpetrated greatness to the concept of time. It is a malediction of the human condition that we have such preoccupation with the categorisation of everything else around us: we harbour a hopelessly enthusiastic desire to define order where the order cannot be. And so, the historical record becomes the chronological detailing of human and inhuman accounts. Our stories are defined in the binary tradition, presenting pivotal moments in a linear continuum, summarised efficiently within key intervals. However, this can be a misleading misalignment of causality because time is an illusionary concept that is relative to position. Position and condition.

Some speak of three times—the past, the present, and the future—while others say there is only one time, our time. For me, though, there is an all-time and a no time, and just so very much time, sometimes. Some of this time, I have spent lingering in the lonely dark of night, seeking the kind of bright clarity that those enduring the yoke of anticipation will often aspire to. How will they depict this time? I wonder, how, indeed, in their clear and concise terms? Will they write of us choking our last breath in the carbon-filled atmosphere of industry and commerce as we clamber for a foothold to watch what once had been steadily sinking into murky in-transience? I suppose we will all know in time... or not.

It is rare for me to wonder at such things. I never really was the kind of person to seek great answers or great questions of great significance, great deeds, great wars, for instance. Just small curiosities with small agencies: instrumentality and causality. I've only ever wanted to know why. Textbook case.

So, in that small crevice of a shelter carved out in the barren and uncongenial environment that was now the world around me, after the event, that is, well, I fastened my attention quite closely to the past. Before this, of course, I had only dared to look ahead.

You would find me there still, being all closely attentive to the past, in the past, sat within the past tense if it were not for the perseverance of him, the husband, my husband. Some days, I could thank him, but some days, I could not.

I should describe him, the husband, for the sake of character development. However, I must warn you that I lack objectivity in the matter. He is a bear-like fellow, the husband, large and tenacious, having a firm foothold in the here and now and very little sense for sensibilities, although he labours hard to improve what he considers to be his limited understandings of emotional complexities. Try as he might, he could not fully comprehend his wife's decision, my decision, for separation but decided early on to apply all the dogged determination and persistent pertinacity to the situation, which is his natural continence anyway. This is just his way.

It was a resolution that he sought—a resolution to what was a clear irregularity of an otherwise quite perfect life. He was happy enough. We were happy enough. With that aim, the restoration of said happiness, that is, he would come to visit every day that I would allow, and if not permitted contact in this form, then would conduct it in some other way, but daily, nonetheless.

He was relentless, but it was an obstinacy born from a limitless well of unfathomable compassion rather than some belligerent sort of rejection or refusal.

Like Woolf's Mrs. Ramsay alone by her window: a two-dimensional character, the projection of someone else's mind, animated only in the ontology of some other being. Distant. I had withdrawn into a place inside myself. Spent and arid is how I was. That internal well of abundance and profusion, which focussed so intently on the needs of those around, was entirely parched. There was nothing left to give, and my solace resented any intrusion that would require even a modicum of energy, any scratching of willpower because there was little enough to get through the day as it was.

Truthfully, I took umbrage at the assault on my already stretched resources, but nevertheless, for his sake, I clung to what we once were and tried hard to make this a sort of reality. And when he came, he brought such expectations. Because ultimately, despite the determination of this ursine being, all that strength of purpose seems to arise almost entirely through what he perceives as my own inexhaustible resilience. I think this may be the way of a marriage or partnership such as ours that we derive strength from one another.

In some parts of myself, I knew this then, too, but was unable to view myself in any such terms. This, this person I was, this was a creature of inadequacy, feeble and defective. I saw only the victim and viewed myself through a lens distorted by loss and despair. But he brought forth a sense of endurance that I came to rely upon and rely upon now. We all need something of endurance in a world so inherently unendurable.

Perhaps what I am trying to say is that he is always faithful, my husband, even when I have no faith left in him or in myself. His ardent faith remains burning true, bright, and constant, and it was this, his conviction, that gradually reignited my prevailing spirit. But then, sometimes, in the face of his forced positivity, I would feel myself slipping away, watching as if from somewhere else, going through the motions of living while quietly remaining in the comforting cavern of my melancholy.

Almost soothed now by the embrace of unhappiness, slumped, despondent, and heavy-hearted, not seeing a path back to the world that I had once inhabited.

No man is an island, but sometimes a woman can find herself adrift.

'Anxiety, depression, and stress' was the physician's diagnosis after the allotted ten minutes of evaluation time. He advised me to spend some time at rest and printed a prescription for tiny round blue tablets with an array of side effects that would counteract any potential benefit, or so it seemed at the time. After all, he assumed it was related to my job, and things were unlikely to improve in terms of these personal circumstances. We all have to do our bit. Medication could be a convenient way of uplifting the mood so that at least work performance may continue unabated after a little time away from the desk, of course. This was either what he said or what I understood.

When you think about it, how could a person not be suffering from low mood when faced with the prospect of a seemingly unlimited lifetime in virtual chains to an ergonomically fully adjustable desk chair, which would slowly compress their vertebrae until the long-awaited, dreamed-of, and saved for retirement period which was then spent in traction and a spinal support programme? I took the pills.

I thanked the man because this was the right thing to do. You always thank the man. But also, because from within these waves of wretchedness, the few minutes of state-funded health care and accompanying prescription for state-endorsed pharmaceuticals seemed like some kind of a solution. Of course, the confines of that all-encompassing fear would not allow for a disclosure close to any form of authenticity, but what would be the point anyway? There was no physician's flowchart for this particular problem and certainly no state-funded treatment plan. So, instead, I gladly agreed with the identification of the soulless office job for this most recent despondency. Indeed, the physician himself was subject to an inconceivable mountain of bureaucracy and performance-related targets and openly pondered how long it would be before his own similar conditions of employment would warrant a long-term sick note. It was easy to empathise with such a predicament in his patients. As I left, he called for the next with a sort of weary resignation.

Later, stood in line at the bright white, overly sterile chemist, my mind screamed out for a return to the routines—but once you've been there, once you've reached the precipice of your inner consciousness, once you've looked your demons right in the eye and slipped off that cliff into bleak, dark, engulfing despair, then there is never a path back up. If the terrors of the mind, those that dwell in the recesses of our consciousness, may materialise at any given moment, then there is no safe place to be. No longer merely fodder for our dreams, those sly memories that we try to suppress with hard spirits and suspicious-looking cigarettes, well, nobody wants confirmation of their authenticity. Humankind has not invented narcotics powerful enough to deflect the fallout when those particular personal souvenirs get loose, and although some try, they usually find that however potent the substance is, it may only offer some temporary relief from what will inevitably become a lifetime of anguish and torment.

When you open that door, there is just no shutting it again, and I knew with a great sense of impending doom that the only way from here was down. Pills or no pills.

But despite all that, and with the solution in place: prescription and rest, I packed up my books and clothes and things and left the small yellow brick house, returning to the scene of my most recent crime. Knowing by now that they could come anywhere, anytime, anyplace, and that the big white door with its big strong locks would do nothing to prevent them. Still ever vigilant, though, I spent my days by the window, watching and waiting. And sometimes, when all that watching and all that waiting became too much, then I would drive out far away in that shiny, blue hatchback and sob until the hollow well inside was empty again. Then, when there were no tears left to cry, I would freshen up that smile and head back home.

Home. There was a kind of clumsy awkwardness to being where I had already been. The husband, my husband, was unsure of how to present his support, so he decided on a sort of demonstrative advocacy that was directed into focused and frenzied activity. He bustled and whirled around like a storm in a teacup as I sat watching, trapped in a vortex of my own making. One by one, the rooms that I had known so well became subtly different as he decorated and furnished, like applying an overlay of bright gloss paint to an older peeling surface. He was hoping to inspire some new purpose, some new intention, some new ambition in his slowly subsiding wife. But I struggled to consider a future or even a present as all around began to spin wildly out of focus.

'Happy?' he would enquire.

'Mmmm?' I would respond, irritated at having had my contemplations interrupted.

Of course, I would not have even the faintest idea if I were happy or not happy or what I might feel instead. And it became increasingly difficult to find excuses to cover up for this lack of awareness of the here and now, and of the happy or not happy situation. So, to avoid unnecessary intrusions into my reflections, then I would just lie. Simples. I'm happy. Of course, I'm happy. Happy. Happy. Happy. Smile. Might just have a laydown. Big smile. Doctor's orders.

If you want to be left alone, then just smile and look happy. Tip for you there.

IV

NOM SUM QUALIS ERAM

(I am not such as I was)

I and my bear-like husband live in a town called Rotherham. I know, right, Rotherham? Rotherham needs little introduction these days, except perhaps to say that it's a town like many other towns, a town made of concrete, damp bricks, and lost hopes. And the fact that there are so many towns just like Rotherham is probably the most worrying thing about it. Keeps me up at night.

Those that make the journey into what locals think of as the actual town, as in the centre of commercial activity. Well, they are met by closed shutters, a stratigraphy of graffiti, and the ambient stench of decay. Because the sprawling settlements representing the collective Rotherham are lined with polystyrene cartons and twisted plastic, the discarded debris of commerce. Just like so many of their neighbouring communities.

You see, the local council responsible for collecting the taxable income of Rotherham's constituents has year on year been fighting with the ever-increasing tide of environmental and economic burdens placed on them, with little in the pot leftover for social and recreational interests. So, Rotherham is one of those towns that has yielded to the burden of national austerity and restraint. Later, this will probably be depicted as some kind of self-immolation by those who decide the historical narrative of such events. A hypothetical Iphigenia: we give so that you may prosper. But Rotherham, too, was once a place of prosperity. Nestled in the Yorkshire countryside, it has previously been described as a powerhouse of the Industrial Revolution, its natural minerals and ores attracting an earlier kind of tradesman and settler. Now, only a forest of LED streetlamps stands tall and proud, once there was an abundance of lush green trees, stretching their thirsty roots downwards towards rich veins of precious black coal and ore. This brought merchants from the south and, with them, bags of silver and gold and promises. Promises were made to poor peasant farmers who thought there could be a better life than working the fields with the sun on their backs and their wives beside them.

Alas, for their children and their children's children. Instead, they crawled deep into the dark, hot dirt, and dug and scraped, and heaved and hauled the bags of rich, shining dusty coal to the surface for their smartly stitched employers. And the air hung heavy around them in thick, dark smog. No longer were there trees to cut but coal to buy, and their wives would walk the stone streets and breathe in the ash of their labour, looking upwards towards the sun and seeing only smoke.

Next came the steel plants, where the coal was used to power the machines to make the alloys to make more machines, and men toiled endlessly in nights as endless as Hades itself, with hot molten liquid splashing and oozing and sparking in bright red scalding ribbons all about. Their wives wept freely as sons came of age and slowly walked into the belly of the beast because they might never know what it was to work in the fields with the sun on their backs and their wives beside them.

In this way, industry revolutionised humanity, it revolutionised Rotherham, and commerce became king. Where once were fields, instead became factories and houses. Row on row of soot-smothered bricks, sheltering families who would cling to the warmth of their coal fires, precious heat purchased with the toil of their backs. Scratching out a living on a landscape of greed, they believed that life was good because this is what they were taught to believe.

So, by the time of the here and now, the year of our commerce, 2010, I and my bear-like husband lived in this town called Rotherham. We, too, scratched and scraped each day like our forebears and those before them. But on the post-industrial landscape of Rotherham and towns like it, where industry had been dissolved and delegated to different countries whose people had not yet acquired the concept of 'Rights' and where the farms and fields had long since capitulated to public housing schemes, then scratching and scraping each day usually involves some kind of customer focussed service.

In this town, which was like so many other towns, the rhythm of daily life revolves around the numbing drudge of routine office-based work. Most people labour most days for wages, and these wages will then be used to purchase the products of their toil at over-inflated prices. Such is it so that the shareholders will become increasingly wealthier, adding wealth upon wealth, and the people who live and work in towns like Rotherham believe that life is good because this is what they are taught to believe.

But when a person no longer believes that life is good, then this becomes a problem. This becomes abnormal, not normal, not the norm. To believe something is not good is to believe that something is bad. We cannot believe that life is bad. Or at least not for long, and not too many of us.

Other people are taught to worry when a person they care about begins to believe that life is not good and that life is bad. We must observe each other for signs because the television tells us so.

When I was no longer driven to strive for new consumer electronics and fashion-branded accessories, for instance, then my husband, well, he knew that something was wrong. Life must have a purpose, and the television told us what that purpose was.

The physician was also a person who worried about my lack of purpose, although he probably wouldn't have put it quite this way himself. Having assessed my development monthly in the allotted ten-minute sessions available to review a patient's medical progress, he had been unable to detect any signs of improvement.

He was a diligent fellow, this physician, who had assumed the life of caring for others because he did exactly that. Please don't think otherwise from the cynicism of my narration. It's merely that he was somewhat perplexed by my situation whilst at the same time being at the mercy of an overarching healthcare hegemony for his diagnostical and medicinal direction.

So, he referred again to his Area Trust guidelines for the next step in the process. Already, he had administered the small blue tablets and prescribed a significant period of absence from the monotonous drudge that employment can represent, as was the agreed protocol. According to his flowcharts, this should have ensured that I received sufficient rest and state-endorsed advertising to have imbued in me that sense of gratuitous gain again. By now, I should have an interest in the prospect of returning to my job and those regular wage-related credits which could be exchanged for the shoes or bags that I loved so much or something else that the marketing gurus at 'Megalamania' had carefully publicised.

It was his job and purpose to keep other people toiling at theirs, so he carefully considered the options available to him and decided on a course of action that was within his small degree of autonomy to deliver. I was to receive six hours of therapy courtesy of the local authority.

They call it the postcode lottery. Something about a lack of resources and funding available in this particular area. Six hours is what we get to make or break a life. There are a lot of broken lives in Rotherham.

'What would you like to talk about today?'

The image flashed momentarily in my mind. Grey, mottled, scratching, diesel. Grease, I gasped, choking. I forget myself sometimes.

'Nothing in particular. It's been good. I've been good. It's been a good week.' Liar. I tell lies. They used to call me a liar, and they were right. I hear them hissing liar as my mouth tells lies. I smiled unconvincingly. Everyone loves that smile. There's that smile, they say. Help. Help me.

'What about your family? Are they supporting you?' 'We speak a lot.' I am not lying now.

It had already started by the time I got home. Squawking, impatiently squawking, furiously squawking, loudly and incessantly squawking. Squawk. Squawk. Squawk. Now. Demanding. Right now. I will not be denied. SQUAWK. Now, my girl, or I'll give you something to cry over.

We sit across from one another on solid surgery chairs padded with good, reassuringly supportive arms and neutral, hard-wearing, wipe-clean fabric. The friendly local therapist employed through the Area Trust talks softly about my job or my old job. The timeline is so blurry now.

MEA CULPA

How my old job had gone so wrong, why I had not been able to continue doing my old job, and why I could not return to my old job. Who gives a shit about my old job?

I sat there with my mind entirely blank, not thinking about my old job, any job, a new job, or jobs in any way, but every now and again, when it seemed appropriate, making some noise that would seem pleasing to the friendly local therapist. And smiling. Gotta love that smile.

People tell me I have great listening skills. I have no idea what they just said. Totally blank.

What kind of new job would you like to do? Where do you see yourself five years from now? What part of your old job did you enjoy best? Fuck knows.

I would sit there blankly and open my mouth, and nice, polite words would sort of fall into and out of it. From where they came, I had not the foggiest. It was like the sounds just bypassed me altogether, or my mind at least, which was now just a vague sort of smoky, tired blank, with nothing in it at all except the flashes of images. Images of grey, mottled, scratching diesel fumes. Images of that night. Choking images of the choke. Images that I could not control, like the words. Get a lid on it.

I was a void, and I was empty, but for the startling images. Was, am?

I looked around, dazed, at the hazy surgery half-light and the high privacy windows while the words fell out of my blank behalf, and I wondered how to form a sentence of my own.

Then, more of the squawking.

'What did you say? What did she say? What did you say about me? Well, what did you tell them?'

SQUAWK. SQUAWK. SQUAWK.

'So, I said… So, she said… are you listening? Oh, charming.' Slam. Squawk. Squawking. Rocking. Crying. Squawking. Screeching.

Being conscientious in my nature, I would arrive early each week for the therapy session, anxious and uncertain but a bit optimistic. I wanted what everyone else seemed to want. I wanted to return to my former self. My former self was a distant figure now. Unrecognisable. That old me bore little resemblance to the wilting girl with the nervous, flicking brown eyes and the dry, thin mouth. This new person was ill at ease away from the familiar confines of those well-known walls, and on tenterhooks, all the while sat within them. I am not such as I was.

I've always been a people pleaser, though, whichever version we're talking about, so I did my very best to convince the friendly local therapist that the therapy was indeed proving successful. But she wanted more than empty platitudes. And I just wanted it to stop. That shrill, persistent squawk, that is, that ceaseless screeching, but when I did give in and supply the required attention if only to stop the demand of it, then there would be the unremitting piercing penetrating titter. It was a no-win situation.

'It just won't stop,' a revelation, even to me. The voice was tentative and unsure. 'How does it make you feel?'

'Exhausted. Drained.'

'What happens if you don't respond.'

'She'll get angry. I don't want to make her angry.' 'Why? Why don't you want to make her angry?'

'Bad things. Bad things happen when she's angry.'

I didn't respond that afternoon. After all, bad things were already happening, and the friendly local therapist pointed that out. And it squawked angrily that day and the next, but I gave it no acknowledgement. Pulled to the limit, like a taut piece of stiff old elastic, which has become crumbled and fragile with age, I resolutely denied it what it craved, and when I arrived early for my therapy session the following week, there was something peeking slightly above the vague sort of tired blank, something small and glinting, something that was a bit more solid and a bit prouder, something a bit unsure, but there nonetheless, and rather than the words just falling from my mouth, I let that small, glinting object give those words some direction. And the therapist sighed with relief. It seemed to me, at the time, she felt like we were finally getting somewhere. Maybe that's what she said.

So it was that I moved a little way, a small way forward from the void, like a tentative young fawn standing on long, spindly legs, nervous and staying close to the point of safety. I should mention that I take solace in the poetry of the ancients. Homeric metaphor. Euripidean infanticide. All of this has happened before, and all of this will happen again.

Anyway, the point that I'm trying to make is that it had not been a conscious decision, a thought-out plan, a decisive action but a sort of force of momentum that had given me a kind of torque that led to action. I have no idea where it came from.

It was on that same day, or shortly after that day, or somewhere around that time, that in some ultimate act of rebellion, I contacted the telephone service providers and had my telephone numbers changed, ultimately eradicating the threat of that incessant squawking from my life forever, or at least for now. Quite literally the bravest thing that I have done in my whole life. Fuck bungee jumps.

Having brought me into the world, she feels that this relatively unremarkable contribution warrants a lifetime of familial devotion, regardless of her own actions or endeavours. But the persistence, the imperative, and the extremity of her demands back then was nothing short of an exploitation of my unfortunate predicament, which the friendly local therapist, from her objective standpoint, could quite clearly decipher. You will never judge me harsher than I judge myself.

Anyway, after this tiny act of liberation from a life of servitude, I was left whirling, unsure what the new horizon would look like over the metaphorical hill of healing. But I still felt at this time that my mother would surely understand because mothers love their daughters, and this is something that everyone knows for sure and is taught at a very early age from the world around. So, I continued with small but remote tributes like flowers and chocolates but could not bring myself to make the arduous eighty-mile journey to visit in person for reasons that remain beyond my comprehension. There was no question of them coming here. '*If you command the terrain, then you will have the advantage,'* said Sun Tzu in The Art of the War.

This was an interesting breakthrough, as far as the friendly local therapist was concerned anyway, so she used her discretion to secure some additional sessions and then asked the inevitable question, 'Tell me about her. Tell me about your Mother.' But I was left reeling at this because, of course, I am not supposed to talk about my family and had already contravened every rule I knew by rejecting their chronic and persistent intrusion into my daily affairs. And although I wanted to be pleasing, I worried what bad things would happen as a result of my disclosure. I worried about what form of retribution my loving mother would take.

You have no idea what it's costing me to write these things down. Even now.

V

SI VIS AMARI AMA

(If you want to be loved, love)

Some stories do not have a natural starting point or a resolute end. Some stories just come into being. They materialise from a complex set of circumstances into a backdrop of continuous composition; they are episodic, intermittent, and incidental, at least towards the broader sequence of events.

It was from just such a progression that this small and somewhat unfortunate chain of happenings emerged. Like a small ripple in already stormy waters, almost indiscernible amid the wider chaos. Depending, of course, on how closely you looked. But for the purpose of applying some systematic chronological order to what would otherwise be in disarray, we will begin here at the point of the progenitor, roughly the place of inception.

My mother. My mother loves her stories. Long stories, short stories. Stories passed through quiet hissed

45

breath between taut pink lips as her small brown eyes darted pensively from side to side, guarding against some intrusion or other. Stories are her gems.

Now the story goes that my mother had been an awkward young girl. All dark hair and thick dark glasses with clumsy shoes and a sort of unkempt, shambolic appearance that was unusual by comparison to that of her more presentable peers. I can vouch that even into middle age, she remained a short but determined creature, with two small brown eyes that would fix at their target with piercing precision and set the hair on the backs of their neck, standing straight to attention.

She was the kind of person who could make a grown man feel acutely uncomfortable in ways that he could never understand, but not in a provocative sort of manner, more like how a person might feel when they catch a glimpse out of the corner of their eye of some large and crawling arachnid. She was unsettlingly malevolent at times but could be sickeningly sycophantic at others, and it was difficult to tell which was the worse. It was also difficult to tell when she might strike.

Truth be told, she always carried with her a sense of

loneliness and isolation that comes with being that bit different. Desperate to belong but never really understanding how, she spent her time on the sidelines of other people's lives, looking wistfully in. It was this sense of longing that gave rise to so many of those other harder and sharper sensitivities that she bore. It might have helped her to know that the strange sort of empty yearning deep inside was something that most of us encounter from time to time when we're just in need of a little reassurance. But she wasn't the sort who could put a name to these kinds of things or understand a look of pining in some other being.

So, jokingly, at family gatherings and such, they used to say that she'd been born with frown lines already in place because that was how she mainly appeared: scowling into photographs. Over time, she learned to smile a little, though, and you could see these changes occurring in those old black-and-white stills. This small compromise appeased her anxious and overbearing mother, whom I would later know as my grandmother.

When a boy at school looked her way, well, this was when the real trouble started because she immediately thought that all her prayers had been answered, and the unsettling need that threatened to consume her was finally defeated. Throwing caution to the wind, she jumped straight in, and after this, they needn't bother reminding her to adjust the curvature of those thin, taut lips as she stared gloomily at the lens because a euphoric disposition came over her in some natural way.

Most people know the course of young love has a tendency not to run smoothly. Nevertheless, this does not stop those fresh-faced fledglings barely out of pigtails from building up hopes and dreams around a young man of their liking, and before you know it, then there are tears and tantrums because the young man has not lived up to their overly romanticised expectations. After all, this is a lot of pressure for a person to process with such a small amount of experience, on top of the other things in life that they might be expected to deal with, like the burden of overly intensive parents and decisions that will affect the adult version of themselves that they are yet to meet. Needless to say, the boy did not respond well to another woman trying to manipulate his time and affection, and soon afterward the relationship ended before it had even started. So, of course, the young girl's happiness and dreams came crashing down around her, as so many others had crashed before.

People can react in different ways to a situation like this. Disappointment may drive some to a period of deep and mournful self-reflection, for instance, while there are others who pull together all that rejection, hurt, and despair into one big ball of bristling energy and apply this to some new project, reaping in the success of their endeavours, and leaving all the pain and misery of circumstance long behind them. But now, this requires a kind of self-assuredness that the girl who became my mother would never possess. Being as things were, she was never the type to look for answers within. No, she did not take any form of negativity well and tended to indulge in a little self-pity and exaggerated sorrow at even the smallest of calamities, but more than anything, she just could never take any form of refusal, however kindly it might be made.

So that same afternoon, she plotted and planned, waiting for the opportunity, then swallowed what she judged would be just enough small, chalky, bitter-tasting tablets so as to give herself a very uncomfortable stomachache and feeling of apathy. Full of expectation, she then waited patiently in her parents' quiet suburban red brick, carefully arranged by the large bay window because this was where she would be most widely noticeable. Content for a while at least, knowing for sure that the day would be a climatic one because whatever happened next, the boy would be made sorry for what he'd done, and she would finally have the sort of close attentiveness from those around that she so intensely craved.

So much of our lives are open to chance events, wondrous coincidences, and unforeseen happenings. When faced with such improbability and impossibility, it is not too surprising that we should choose to reject the risks and ascribe instead the matter of that most infinite of relationships to a form of serendipity, a divine spirit, to a god. At least through the act of worship and prayer, we may delude ourselves into believing that we can induce the omniscient being of our choice and creation to act on our behalf and positively influence subsequent fortunes. All praise to God, for he offers comfort to us in our times of trouble. For others, though they live at the will of an unintentional sort of destiny, their lives are shaped forever by the fluttering of a butterfly's wing, the strange winds of fate, the chaotic, disorderly order of causality.

That day, her small and persevering father, my grandfather, came home from work a little earlier than usual to find his eldest daughter heavily lethargic in a living room chair with an empty bottle of sleeping tablets resting in her lap. He immediately phoned for an ambulance, and outside, a large bright Lepidoptera twitched gently in the evening breeze.

This is not one of my mother's stories. Whether through guilt, shame, or some such reason, she never talked about that summer afternoon. In fairness, a long time passed before any of them would talk about it, and when they finally did disclose the carefully buried secrets of their long-forgotten past, they spread them out like tiny breadcrumbs given to the birds.

You never did get a full picture, only scraps, and it was difficult to say which parts had been artfully reworked in the passing of all that time.

They told me that as she sat in the hospital bed that night, her stomach dredged of all toxicity and her face burning red with righteous indignation, she was wild with grief for the act of living. They say that she made a sort of peace with death that day and waited quietly like a good girl should for it to sweep in and take her away. But I know from my own experience that she has some artistry when it comes to putting on a performance, and I think this may have been the start of the show. The prologue.

They blamed the boy, of course, because no mother and father could easily accept a part in their child's suffering, and she couldn't look them in the eye and clearly and concisely say exactly what was troubling her. The physicians milling around, well they had their ideas by this point at least, but the family would not hear of any talking therapy or medication, and this was a different time when nervous sorts of troubles were washed away with mugs of sweet tea and inspirational mutterings and brushed quickly under the rug, so none could see.

I think it was the fear of condemnation, the muttering

voices, and stolen glances that compelled them not to act. Don't get me wrong, they kept a good eye on her, a quick, sly sideways eye, or horse eye, as they used to call it in some northern parts, but her mother, well, she convinced herself that all the girl needed was a companion, and she told that boy what for. And the boy felt the weight of guilt about him and so yielded himself to its yoke of an unwanted relationship.

Now, some may question whether or not serendipity had anything to do with the outcome of that fateful day, and I certainly could not say for sure, having not been there at the time. But her mother swore that the girl would never try and gain attention in this manner, and she would not be persuaded otherwise. Of course, she would not be the first young girl, and sad to say, she will not be the last, who in a desperate attempt for others to see their pain and outrage, will go to any lengths to achieve just some particle of consideration, and it is fair to say, from that point onwards, those around became ever more attentive and worrisome towards any friction brought towards her. But, whether by chance or circumstance, the event certainly could not be said to have worked in her favour because that day, she had the opportunity for some real kind of help and relief from what ailed her. And the chance just passed her by. I mourn for this girl, for the life that could have been. If you want to be loved, love. That's my advice. Oh, that she would take it.

So, in this way, she got what she wanted but not what she needed. The boy came back. He didn't come back of his own volition, though, and it was soon obvious that he had a wandering heart to match his wandering eye. But she was young, and the world was still full of hope and possibility, so she set her mind to what she wished for and decided on a way that she could make it happen. In her soul's eye, in the quiet place of contemplation, that inner reserve of solitude and searching, well, in that place that we all go to in the quiet of the night when no one is there watching, in that small place inside herself she built a little world, a world that she fully intended to make real. But the problem was that the boy had dreams too, and try as she might, she could never quite persuade him towards the version of existence that she had so lovingly and carefully prepared for them deep inside her mind. His dreams were always bigger than her own, you see. They could not be contained in the small, quaint picture that she carried inside herself, and she mourned already, knowing that he would soon be gone again and she would be left all alone. But soon, she found a solution in the way that some girls do, when they are in some low and needy place, thinking only of how to prevent the pain in their fragile hearts from shattering their worlds into slivers of thin glass across a hard slate floor. What she did, she did to protect herself and that hard, dark little soul of hers.

When she was later asked what happened or how this arose, she always had a different version of events, a carefully crafted, manufactured, illustrated version that would fit the occasion, depending, of course, on who was doing the asking.

For some, it was the physician at fault and an act of conscientious objection due to their faith in a good book and a good lord.

'Well now, if it wasn't for that doctor, none of this would have happened,' she would state with fervour and indignation, and most around would believe that she was wronged. 'I asked for contraception, but she refused to give it to me!'

In other cases, she was pressed by an overconfident boy who wouldn't take no for an answer. 'I was frightened of losing him,' she'd offer tearfully, and how they would sympathise that a good, innocent spirit like this was clearly seduced by his roguish charms.

Either way, she always claimed that there had been a firm and uninterrupted belief in marriage anyway, so what difference would a few months and a piece of paper really make?

So, in this way, she sat that day blushing wildly, feeling suddenly small and insecure while she explained what had happened to her parents in words that she had rehearsed a hundred times, watching the colour drain quickly from their faces as they began to prepare a narrative for those around who would surely talk behind twitching curtains and ask what kind of house they kept. She fiercely rejected any suggestions to abort the baby. I was wanted, yes, wanted, needed even. A child would mean salvation. For my mother, a child meant a home of her own, which would mean he could never leave. And secretly, she dreamed of a little girl who would love her like no other and be her best friend forever.

The boy, my father, told his parents in the quiet comfort of their middle England and then watched as they wept for his future. And he watched as they wept for his missed opportunities also. And he continued to watch, the time ticking slowly onward, as they wept for the life that he could have had.

His own father then turned a moment from his despair to insist on marriage because it was the right thing to do, the decent thing to do, and he was nothing if not a right and decent man. At this, the full enormity of the situation slowly began to sink into that once young and carefree mind, and so the boy, the boy who was to be my father, well, he began to weep too. And this was how the girl, the girl who was to be mother, well, this was how she finally won her bitter prize.

VI

QUALIS MATER, TALIS ET FILIA

(As is the mother, so is her daughter)

Not all stories are nice stories. But stories are ubiquitous to the family anyway, nice or not. Interesting assortments of well-rehearsed oral traditions that get brushed down and laid out for some special occasion or other. Shared about, like home-made delicacies, because these family stories are more than just some entertaining yarn to pass a dull afternoon gathering. No, these stories serve as a kind of collective narrative that helps each new generation understand who they are, how they should behave, and where their responsibilities lie. These kinds of folk tales are as old as time itself, older in fact. Wherever groups of people collect, so too will groups of carefully woven, sometimes whimsical, always creative, shared chronicles that unite the collaboration into the cohesive, self-contained social units you see before you. What defines us, as in the collective us, is the stories that hold that 'us' together. What defines them, as in the collective them, is the stories that set 'them' apart.

So even the most maladaptive of families have their very own superised legends, rehearsed with a glazed look and tearful gaze to an enthralled audience, who then pass down these traditions to others in a very similar way. Whether or not they're true is really neither here nor there because the only important part of the story, in fact, the only essential element to the story, is the very act of telling it.

Now, this is how I learned the narrative of my birth. You remember me, of course; I was kneeling on the floor behind the door when fear settled in on the floor beside me. Well, long before that night, that night of shocking, violent, inescapable realisation, long before all of that happened when I was still running, still chasing, still creating a world and not crumpled, breathless in the remains of my last one, long before that night I had listened to the collective stories of my family, retold and reworked, time and time again. Well, if I'm honest, and I'm trying hard to be honest here, then you should know that I have probably read a little between the lines and then developed my own assumptions about where I came from, how I fit in, and who I am. And this is how that story goes:

The girl and her boy, my mother and my father, they remained in an uneasy relationship, living in my maternal grandparent's house, with him disappearing as often as he could and the girl making up excuses to those around her for the obvious failing in their very short matrimony, then rattling that red-hot temper on any that dared to disagree.

As it turned out, summer came especially early that year, and it soared into record temperatures, which did nothing to dispel her short fuse or heightened anxieties. Being a married woman didn't mean much since she was living in a small, cramped, pink polyester double at the front of her parents' family home, with her younger sister still at school and an elderly dependent grandparent close by, too. Tensions were running high.

You see, that dream she'd held onto, that girlish whimsy of her own home and her own husband, with ivy growing around a small wooden door and a baby playing in the garden, well, it was really a dream of independence that she'd been harbouring. Still, with her small mind and her small ways, she just hadn't thought of another method to achieve it. The reality of a heavy pregnancy, little or no money, and a narcissistic mother in the bedroom next door were as far removed from the quaint idea she'd held of a grown-up life as just about anything could ever be. In fact, she was lonelier now than ever. The boy was gone for most of the time, leaving her outcast: too young to make friends with any other mothers-to-be and too pregnant to meet up with any of the schoolyard pals she'd once known. She isolated herself in a prison of her own shame and refused to leave the house. You really have to feel for this kid.

As the heat drove upwards, her mood plummeted, but finally, she found herself an answer. Her baby would be born soon, and then she would have someone to always love and need her, a companion for life who would fill that raw, empty space that was so wretched with need of a little affection. My heart aches for this girl.

The due date coincided with her own eighteenth birthday, and slowly, her mood started to lift as the voices whispered excitedly in her ear, gathering tempo and earnestly making plans for her future. This child would become her best friend, her ally, the kind of support that she had always longed for, and they would do everything together. Carefully, new dreams were born, different kinds of dreams, and she clung hopefully to this new vision of wholeness, with no one around noticing or questioning this strange intent. Even now, I wish it had worked out better for us.

So, as she looked forward to this birthday coming, she would quietly tell the bump that this was the day it should be born. She had decided that they would start their new life together, and expectantly, she made the necessary preparations while all around her waited in eager anticipation, seduced against all logic by the surety of her announcements. But nature does not submit easily to someone else's timetable, and as accustomed as she was at this point to getting what she wanted, it did not turn out as intended. When the day came and went, she was outraged. Hot, heavy, and bitterly disappointed that this daughter had failed to appear, that she had let her down already and not yet even in the world. Well, it was here that she began to suspect that this small person may prove to be just like the rest, and the voices tittered around, fuelling those apprehensions. For the first time, she began to have doubts over this life-altering course of action while all around looked on with softness in their eyes and commented with fondness on how keen she was to become a mother. It was this bitter disappointment that later seemed to symbolise our relationship rather than that earlier anticipation. I wish it could have been different.

The child that she had planned and pained for repeatedly refused to comply with what she deemed to be perfectly rational and reasonable demands, which were often first discussed within the protective secret circle, her very own personal inner associates, or else petitioned upon her by them, after some transgression or other.

Now, my perspective on the matter is not objective, but from personal experience and observations made by others, it seems to me that my very own mother dearest tried to bring life into the world to serve only her own selfish desires. Of course, when it came to filling the gaping void of vulnerability that inspired her determination, she found that life, or me, was lacking in almost every way imaginable.

Being the giver of life does not automatically extend the right to demand a degree of dependence from said offspring or to confine the right to autonomy. It was this very right, this self-born right to self-governance, that my mother could never really tolerate because she saw the world and all those in it only as the constructs of her own somewhat over-enthusiastic mind. After all, it is what the voices told her.

From the stories that my mother told me, where she would refer to herself and myself in the third person, like she was describing some distant familial scene in her head, a sitcom perhaps or something she had read in a book, well, it seemed that the disillusionment with motherhood crept in relatively soon, and I sometimes wonder if she had a sort of post-natal depression that was not picked up on. No one would blame a teenager struggling to cope with such overwhelming responsebility, least of all me.

So, the story continues, it was with some

consternation that she discovered my infant self to be even more stubborn in nature than she had first suspected, and when the day finally came, it was two weeks later than she had deemed agreeable. She was both unprepared and overjoyed all at the same time.

Her mother owned a small hairdressing salon close to the family home, the kind lined with long rectangular mirrors that expose the rows of dryer banks, waiting customers, and the misty wisps of hairspray and cigarette smoke hanging like clouds under a low brown ceiling. She had cajoled the girl into spending time there on the pretence of needing an extra pair of hands and the lure of a few precious notes. At nine months pregnant and a little overdue, the girl did little of any real value except sweep the floor from time to time and make the tea, but the customers fussed and pecked around, and it pleased her mother to see a smile on that worried young face.

It was on one of these occasions as the ladies lined up in their designated styling stations. The kettle steamed noisily through the haze of peroxide and cigarette smoke that her waters finally broke in a splash on the floor. She looked up, scared and red, at her mother, who was filled immediately with weary resignation. This was it.

They launched themselves quickly into the small yellow convertible motorcar waiting outside and began the arduous journey to the closest city hospital, where the delivery had been carefully planned by the mature and understanding midwife who had taken close measurements and offered sympathetic glances. As the contractions came, the girl was shaken and confused by the pain that this much-longed-for baby could cause. She was simply not ready for the reality of the birth. At the hospital, as she was wheeled away behind closed doors, her mother paced the corridor, smoking furiously and wondering how they would cope with this new tragedy, this new misfortune, this calamity that had hit their already overburdened family. She called for the boy, but the boy never came. At this point, she thought, it was probably for the best.

They say that the birth was quick and that when the overwrought new grandmother was finally allowed back into the room to visit, well, all those worries, all those anxieties, all those trepidations, they all just eased away because there in the crib next to her tired but happy-looking daughter was a small baby girl dressed in the tiny woollen clothes that had been knitted, stitched, and painstakingly collected. But best of all, amid all this was a shock of the softest, darkest hair she had ever seen. 'Oh Cathy,' she said, with tears in her eyes, 'Are you sure it's Adam's?' and with that, the girl's smile immediately faded and was replaced by a look of contempt and the all too familiar indignation as she began sobbing inconsolably into the starched linen bedclothes. Her mother just turned away and back to the new wriggling life before her, either way, it would all be okay. As for Cathy, this became just another story of how I failed her as a daughter. By bringing about such questions with my untimely arrival and unexpected characteristics.

Cathy stayed in the hospital for a few days while the nurses taught her how to feed the little one, prepare the formula milk, and change the nappies. Despite her attempts to project an outwardly developed appearance and inclination at all times, her immaturity was evident all around. The feeling of resentment she felt towards her mother did not easily dissipate, even though her assurances regarding the baby's paternity had been accepted, and the little girl began to prove her right as the postnatal colouring subtly changed over the next few days. She was angry at the child for the betrayal but tried hard not to show it, at least when anyone else was present, remembering her mother's warning about the possible threat from her in-laws. She did not want to look like a bad mother.

Back at home, she did everything that she could to keep the baby quiet and maintain peace and order in the house, determined that she should show the world that she was capable, the world at this point being, of course, just a small handful of people. She had begun to see the day that her daughter was born as symbolic of her own birth into womanhood, and she purposefully claimed independence, her own right to self-rule. So, she began to express a newly acquired assertiveness whenever the opportunity arose, thinking this was the way to demonstrate her coming of age and the putting away of childish ways. With the stakes set high, she informed the local housing officer that her situation had changed and that she would need a place to live for her growing family much more quickly. This would be her ticket to freedom.

In the small, cramped house, the boy came and went, making his excuses. He had been offered a place at university and intended to take it anyway, leaving his wife and child behind, but promised to be home at the weekends and any other time that it was possible. He assured them that he was thinking of them all and the future they would have together, but she just snarled sideways at him and secretly agreed with the voices that he had probably found some other girl, some other bed to sleep in. When he moved towards the child, swaddled in her small white crib, the family terrier that sat beside it growled menacingly, baring his yellow fangs. The boy would shrink back quickly, as the girl laughed at both reactions but never intervened. They all agreed that the small brown dog must be protecting the child and instinctively knew something of the boy's character that had previously been incomprehensible. She cursed herself for that poor judgement, and from this point on, he only saw his daughter from a distance, in someone else's arms. He felt disconnected, like living a waking dream, unable to fully process the magnitude of this new life and his responsibility towards it. He had no clear and determined role. At university, he was just like everyone else, but here in this house, he lived a life that he was unprepared for and hadn't wanted, he was living someone else's version of himself. He felt conflicted and confused, and his health began to suffer.

On one of his rare visits back to their stiflingly polyester-clad room, they argued again about money, a regular sort of discussion, as she secretly harboured the notion that he should be out working to give her what she wanted, instead of idling away his days in study. She carefully treasured all the notes and coins that he brought back to her and secreted them away in a place where only she could find them. When he asked for some back, she became immediately confrontational, panicking that he would take away what she had never had before, distrusting his intentions. The voices prattled away in the background, making their own accusations, and by now, she knew these were the only friends that she could wholly rely on. They suspected it was for drink, card games, and loose women because what else do young men do with their spare time? It was what her mother had told her and what she had seen for herself on the television screen. She was an eighteen-year-old closeted sort of girl and knew nothing more of life than these two infinite sources to which she had considerable access.

It was then that the tenuous string of conformity and obligation that had been holding them together finally and irreversibly snapped, and the boy slumped on the edge of the raspberry-pink bedspread with his head in his hands and sobbed great tears of despair. She looked on at first, dismayed and bewildered by this outburst, unable to empathise, to reach out in understanding at their shared predicament, to offer a tender hand in consolation, or to soothe another's pain. Instead, she turned away and picked up the baby, as much to hide the gaiety that she felt for his sudden expression of emotional suffering as it was to instinctively need the feel and comfort of another. She'd never seen a grown man cry. Gripping the child possessively, Cathy swung back around: 'Just leave,' she said, and her face was full of scorn and derision, contorted into a spiteful smirk, as her eyes danced in the hazy afternoon sunshine. He couldn't look. 'Go.' Her lips were held in a tight, thin line as she struggled to restrain the elation from expressing itself as she spat out the words.

He packed the few meagre things that he had left quickly and phoned his father, who came right away. He knew that she was watching him through the heavily patterned voiles as the motorcar sped away, and he shuddered at the thought. There was something about her face that day, some strange look that he had not quite fully encountered before, something that filled him with a crude sort of creeping fear that he would never forget. He knew this had been a lucky escape.

As the girl watched him leave, the voices rustled in her ear. It had been unexpected, although not to those around. She had baited him as an opportunity to let off steam, to vent the frustrations of another boring day spent in the company of older relatives and a crying child. She had not been able to understand his distress, but she considered her response an appropriate one. She knew now that there was nothing left of the boy that she had met, with the wave of auburn red hair that shone in the sunshine like leaves on a bright autumn day, but she thought that maybe some time away would return him to his senses. It had been a long while since she had seen his wide-open smile and since he had held her in his arms, and she had shared her small dreams and fancies, those wishing well hopes.

If he didn't return, then that was just as well because she saw nothing now but snivelling ineptitude when she looked at him, and it made her stomach knot with fury to think that she had cast all her faith onto this sinking ship. Let him leave, let this boy go, because she had been reborn a woman, stronger and more determined than ever before, and she had no need of him now. She clung to the baby and cried slow tears into the warm bundle gurgling before her. His eagerness to break free had hurt her in a way that she wouldn't be able to name or reckon, but it didn't matter because she was not alone. She had someone who would always love and need her and be her best friend forever. Yes, the voices said, he is a liar and a cheat. "Poor Cathy left holding the baby."

As is the mother, so is her daughter, and she went downstairs and sat sobbing at the kitchen table, as she had seen her mother do so many times before, pitying herself and the life that she had made, waiting for her

MEA CULPA

family to gather around with their condolences.

VII

SEMPER IDEM

(Always the same)

She was ever the foolish one my mother, but then we are a foolish kind of species. For all our technological advancements, scientific discoveries, innovation, revelations, and all that humankind has achieved, it remains a sad and disheartening truth that each new generation seems resolute on wasting their delicate, flimsy existences, repeating the same mistakes as the last. I guess that this is just the human condition, to toil endlessly in one direction and so forever have our back turned towards an alternate path of possibility. We fritter away new opportunities with each rising and passing of the sun.

This is how it was to be for my mother anyway, who, despite having listened to her own mother's woes so often and for so long that she could recite them easily to any who would listen well before her tenth birthday, well despite this, she had gone and got herself into the exact same situation, and of her very own free will. Ever the foolish one.

What we want is not always what we need, and in this case, she had pursued a very particular kind of destiny with forceful determination and furious purpose. And now she was reaping the rewards. Only in hindsight, what had once seemed like a vision of nirvana was, in reality, a young girl's torment because what remained the case was that she was simply a troubled teenage girl who now had the burden of responsibility for another new life. Children raising children, in my opinion, rarely turns out well. I am not referring to physical age.

Now, despite the mutterings of an occasional more reasoned argument, which might from time to time develop the confidence to raise its head above the parapet, so to speak, she was resolved to continue forth, and no one would have talked her round. My mother was always headstrong; truth be told, she liked to play the martyr, too. So, when people found that the boy had left, they assumed that he had just been a bad one because

Joan, my grandmother, made sure that her girl was beyond reproach. Otherwise, it would have looked bad on the family, and she would never have stood for that. They would mutter, 'Poor Cathy, left holding the baby,' as my mother walked past, all lost and forlorn. Or at least this is what she told me 'they' said, but it could have easily been the voices in her head because she was never too sure about the difference. Knowing my mother, well, she would have pinched her lips straight in a thin, self-righteous line, held her head up high, and near on glowed in the light of this self-perceived respect and adoration.

She had been one of those teenage girls who struggled to carve out her own kind of identity, having an unavailable sort of self-involved mother who more or less assigned characteristics to her children rather than waiting for them to develop some interesting and unique traits of their own. Yes, Cathy, my mother, never really could forge a strong sense of who she was and tended to define herself in terms of who she was closest with, instead adopting the most appropriate behaviours to that role. Well, now she had a baby and a pram and some self-derived status, if you like, she knew herself as "mother," "mum," "mummy," and this gave her something to cling to, some raft to hold onto in the rapid and changeable waters of her life.

What was more, though, the small, squirming, wrinkly bundle that she proudly pushed before her attracted attention and a certain degree of consideration, the like of which a new and weary mother might receive from their older, wiser counterparts. Despite all this, though, being stuck at home holding the baby, so to speak, soon began to lose its charm, or at least this is the impression I gleaned from those little moments of quiet revelation. She would repeatedly ask her mother to mind me a little while she had a rest or some time to herself. Now Joan, my grandmother, had never considered herself a maternal sort of woman; she was always upfront and honest about this. She had a soft spot for her baby granddaughter with the beautiful head of hair, and she was always upfront and honest about this, too. Still, Cathy had chosen this life, and Joan was adamant that her daughter would clean up her own mess. Having been a teenage mother herself, she had some understanding of the overwhelming strain that could be associated with caring for a family, but she was finally in a position to break free. She didn't need to be saddled with any more troubles.

'Cathy,' she said, 'you've made your bed, and now you'd better lie in it' because that's what her mother had said to her. Cathy was none too happy about this response, always being one who relied heavily on the assistance of others for any form of chore. It is in my mother's nature to react strongly to the resistance of others to her will and wants. She is a difficult woman, and I'm guessing she was no different when she was younger. Anyway, I think as a result of my grandmother's small opposition, she decided to do just that, make her own bed that is. And when the offer of the council flat came, she immediately accepted and then made her announcement with smug satisfaction, expecting and hoping for some battle from the older woman, some sign of her ongoing affection. Unfortunately, the ploy backfired, and the family promptly began to make plans for her departure as she sat snuffling into the baby's bedclothes, wondering why she was so unloved.

"Poor Cathy," the voices hissed, and she felt dejected

and alone again. She was starting to see the small bundle next to her as the reason for these fresh and hard-hitting rejections. I suppose by now, she was starting to feel somewhat trapped in the life of her own making.

Like so many people, all this young girl needed was to feel a deep and stable connection in her life, to feel the kind of warmth and belonging that comes from a strong, secure, and unshakeable bond that a child develops with their primary caregivers. But having never fully developed this attachment, she had reached a place where, much to the confusion of those around her, spurned any reflection of her parents' partiality towards her and, simultaneously, hungered constantly for a sign of their fondness. So, with this discord, the relationship between them continued for much of her life, and she was never once able to break free of that want or suspicion. Instead, she leaned on others to fill the vacuum it created, and then when on finding that they too could not tolerate her changeability or give her the infinite bounty of enduring devotion that she craved, she would become even more volatile, as that blankness inside threatened to eat her whole.

Cathy was always the same, as far as I understood it. Headstrong, foolhardy, and never able to take an ounce of responsibility. She fiercely guarded her inner bedlam against any that might come close for fear of what those others on the outside would say against her if they knew what raged beneath in her inner realms. Maybe my grandmother had taught her this shame, to hold those aberrations close and dread the talk of others, when really, she was just in need of a little help, the kind of young girl that is sort of disordered. It would be a fair summation that Joan remained relentless in her concealment of what she believed to be a further disgrace. Instead of accepting circumstances as they were, well, her family just continued onwards, always making efforts to please and, above all, keep it quiet.

So, in the following weeks, they collectively prepared the small upstairs flat, busying themselves in ceaseless distraction, buying bits of furniture and new curtains. They say that my grandfather worked hard but still came home at night and laid out wallpaper strips and painted walls in the appropriate colours that she and Joan decreed. The flat was small but had a garden of its own and was just doors away from the revered family grandmother, my great-grandmother. Cathy felt comforted by the presence of this old matriarch and moved a few things in. Her mother visited the street daily, and the family began to settle into a new routine. I think that my mother enjoyed the freedom and feeling of maturity, at least in those first weeks, and I think they all breathed a sigh of relief, believing that a new chapter had been started.

It soon became obvious that the girl was not coping well with the obligations of running her small hearth and home. She sat lethargic for hours watching an old black and white television or staring into space. She was lost in her thoughts, her private world, her private sanctuary. Meanwhile, the baby cried or just lay listless, knowing now that crying was pointless. Of course, she told me in that strange third-person narrative how I lay crying and then not crying and how she would do the same. Cathy became frustrated and discouraged as the bottles and pots piled around while she scraped dirt from toweling nappies and spooned vegetables through a sieve. She was tired and hadn't expected so much work, but at the same time, she was determined that no one would suspect her, so she put a brave face on things and pretended to be happy. The voices told her what to say and do, and she listened. When visitors came, she met them at her grandmother's home and sat in the kitchen quietly fuming, with her lips pulled back into that thin pink line and her eyes targeted downwards. She resented the fuss they made of the child, with the long brown wisps and the big red cheeks; where was her regard? So, she would sit irritated, sipping her tea and nodding curtly in response. The baby was stealing her thunder.

Finally, her mother maybe sensing something was amiss, put aside the usual excuses and made her way upstairs to the flat, but as she walked through the opaque glass door, she was shocked and disgusted by what awaited. The little home they had worked so hard to make for the girl was barely visible beneath the last few months' dirt, grime, and accumulated debris. Filthy laundry had been abandoned in a corner, and the baby, now a toddler, tottered naked on the floor around it. There were pots piled high, caked and crusty in the sink, and scum coating the bathroom. Her mother immediately opened a window to expel the acrid smell. The baby's bedclothes lay rumpled and yellowing, unwashed and untended, much like everything else.

When she looked in the small living room, she gasped in horror. One of the walls they had so carefully and lovingly papered was smeared with yellow-brown feces, now dried and aging. She swung around quickly. Cathy was red with humiliation and rage. She had told her mother not to come upstairs, but Joan had forced her way inside. 'Mum, she did that,' she said accusingly, pointing towards me. 'I only took my eye off her for two minutes,' she spat, 'and look at what she did.' I never heard the last of how I made her look like a bad mother and ruined a good sheet of paper. My mother slumped in tears, or so the story goes, and the old woman softened slightly towards her. 'I'll take the baby out,' she said, 'get it cleaned, Cathy.' With that, she was off to find something to put on the child, and the girl was left in sullen indignation. Shouldn't she have gone out, while Joan did the cleaning? There was an injustice to this situation that she could not share with others—the baby made the mess, and she was left to clean it. She tried to swallow down these new rising feelings of bitterness and hostility that this latest disparity brought forth and instead got on with the scrubbing.

Poor Cathy, the voices whispered consolatory. They were the only ones who understood. As her mother whisked the baby down the steep stairs, vexation remained as her only companion. This was far from the idealised image of motherhood that she had held in her mind for so long.

We all started calling her this eventually: Poor Cathy. I'm not sure how that happened.

Sometimes things have a way of working out, though, and in some ways, Cathy achieved the sort of attentive close observance that she'd always had a craving for because after seeing the way that she'd been living, well, her mother made special efforts to appear much more frequently. She did so with a disconcerting irregularity that left Cathy in a constant state of hypervigilance and paranoia as the voices hissed their recriminations and denunciations quietly where none could hear. She nodded agreement when no one else was looking. In addition, Joan made very obvious inspections of the small home, peering dubiously into the kitchen and checking on the state of the tiny bedrooms, commenting without refrain if something did not meet with her approval. This sort of scrutiny made Cathy intensely anxious. It was not the kind of attention she had hoped for.

So, under this new and unforeseen pressure, she ensured the toddler was always immaculate, cursing wildly if the child became dirty or if the carefully folded layers she was swamped in became ruffled. At the same time, she made sure that their home was spotless, jumping quickly from her seat if she heard a car outside and busying herself noisily and conspicuously in the kitchen on the off chance that some unwelcome visitor may be approaching down the path.

This state of unusual sensitivity did not go unrewarded or unnoticed, though, and everywhere she went, her efforts received praise and recognition.

'Oooh,' they cooed, 'she keeps her nice, doesn't she?' and the girl would beam with satisfaction as she majestically wheeled that claim to her fame proudly in front with the polished chrome of her Silver Cross pram glinting in the sunlight. Cathy basked in the feeling of approval and acceptance that she had always longed for.

'Oooh,' they cooed as she went by, 'she's a good little mam, ain't she?' 'Yes,' she thought, 'I am.'

Now, all this time, Cathy had been forging ahead with her freshly imagined machinations, cooking up new dreams and intentions, blazing a trail for all around to witness.

Well, young Adam had been left struggling, barely staying afloat in its wake. His parents were none too happy that he'd walked away and discredited the reputation of their family but had some understanding of his distress, and when all was said and done, thought more of their son than to try and send him back to the brink of misery with some girl that seemed intent on ruining his good future. That is not to say, though, they did not encourage him to shoulder up and take some responsibility for his actions, and so his father visited the girl and made some arrangements for a little maintenance to be paid weekly, just between her and him, no need to involve the courts.

'Just for the baby,' she had said through those thin, tight lips that she used when she knew she had the upper hand and could claim all forms of self-righteous indignation available to her, 'I don't want anything for myself.'

So, there, it was settled. But away in the city's big, bright, brazen iridescence, with all its cheap sin and seductive vice, Adam was struggling with the enormity of what had just been, of what he had left behind. The reality of his situation remained stark and unblinking, so when those alluring neon lights called to him with all manner of intoxicating things, he got a taste of forgetting, and he liked it. All the swirling feelings of inadequacy, of insubstantiality, of floundering insufficiency that might normally surface later in life when a man had something of capacity behind him to better shelter the storm, well, they had made a shocking and unexpected entrance on his landscape, and he just needed the quiet desensitisation that only hard spirits can bring. It was rare that he stopped to consider the child back home, rare that he stopped to consider anything.

Cathy, now she'd never been far from the small town that she lived in and never been far from the small family that she was born into, but she felt fit to judge others, and when she heard about these exploits well, judge, she did. And as she shared this new information, in hushed-like tones and moderate voices, with the rest of the clan, well, the old family matriarch, she would sit in her chair and smoke her cigarettes and had little much to say on the subject, which was very much unlike her, to not extend an opinion, as the others looked her way with furtive glances. But there was one time when the girl came to visit, a little more worked up than was usual, complaining, sobbing, and saying all manner of things hunched in misery over the old yellow Formica drop-leaf table, talking about the boy and the position he'd left her in. Well, this woman, who had seen two international wars, one great-grandchild, and the world change around her in indescribable ways, turned around and looked her granddaughter dead in the eye and said:

'Cathy, if you call a sheep a wolf for long enough, then he'll start to believe it.' That was the last she ever said on the matter.

The stately old Lizzie-Anne, clad in her fine armour of mohair twin set and freshwater pearls, had a way of shutting things down dead that earned her both the fear and respect of the other members of the family, who would venerate this old dowager like a ceremonial flagship. She was a monarch, a sovereign, a queen among women, and she called a spade a spade.

Adam never really did have the chance to bond with his child, considering the circumstances of her arrival and how he'd been prevented from getting too close. But he'd try to make the effort to see me from time to time. I think he felt an unfamiliar obligation towards this small pink life while at the same time still unable to process the magnitude of the responsibility that this helpless little person presented. Truth be told, I don't think he knew how to be a father, having only ever known his own to be the stern disciplinarian and breadwinner, that was so common to this other time.

When he visited one afternoon in the holidays, though, Cathy barely recognised him, or so she would say later. He was taller now, maybe not in feet and inches, but certainly in stature. His hair had grown long, and he swished it out of his eyes with a whip of his shoulder. That's the thing that I remember; I can remember the swish.

He brought a few crinkled notes, some of the much discussed and long debated maintenance, and sat by the fire playing with my wooden toys. I think it might have been a train or building blocks. Something like that.

In his dark leather jacket and flared trousers, he looked different, older and sophisticated to my mother anyway, and she'd been by herself for some time, focussing on the role of motherhood and keeping house. She blushed lightly and tried to get his attention because she was just a young woman when all was said and done, and she still felt what a young woman would. She would say this later, eyes glazed and looking far away.

When he only seemed interested in playing with the child by the fire, then she thought it best to try and send me away. So, he placed the money on the mantlepiece and made to leave. Cathy stalled him with an awkward conversation about their future, in which she presented the opportunity of there being one and he tried gently to let her down, after which he couldn't leave quickly enough and hastily clumped down the staircase. The girl was left feeling ashamed and brazen, with that familiar feeling of dismissal rising in her chest, followed closely by hot fury and explosive anger as she kicked the wooden train across the floor. At the same time, I cried loudly in the corner, afraid and unsure. The voices comforted and cajoled Cathy as she sank into a nearby chair.

When her mother came later to see how the appointment had gone, she saw that tear-stained face and was immediately alarmed, pressing her daughter for information. Finally, Cathy alluded to some violence, saying he had punched her hard, but in the stomach, so that others wouldn't see the bruising. Her mother was shocked and angry but believed the lies easily. After all, her marriage was marked by the ceaseless animosity of domestic abuse, and so she had come to expect that this would be the same in most relationships. When she discovered from her daughter that this had happened before, underneath her own roof, well she was livid. She would not have that boy come back again while her daughter was alone and unprotected. So, from that point on, the girl's father would accompany her every visit and sit feet away with a fixed expression of open hostility towards the boy, who felt an already uneasy scenario becoming even worse.

So, it was that he just stopped visiting at all. After the decree absolute had been issued, then his father would sometimes appear with the source of the girl's new obsession, the precious maintenance, which she would immediately take to the local shopping centre and spend on new dresses and shiny polished shoes for the child.

'She has nothing for herself,' they would say as she brought the bags home, and again, she would smile contentedly, elated by her victory, because those same people would be later whispering in hushed tones and sideways glances about the boy and what they thought he'd done or not done.

VIII

MENS REGNUM BONA POSSIDET

(His own desire leads man)

"They fuck you up, your Mum and Dad," or so the poem goes. "Man hands down misery to man. It deepens like the coastal shelf [...] don't have any kids yourself."

We moved around a lot when I was growing up, but when I'm laid in the dark at night, staring at the wall, waiting with some small amount of desperation for the sweet relief of sleep, well, it is often one particular house to which I will return. A tiny two-bedroom semi-detached that the council had been kind enough to offer. Oh, how my mother primped and preened. Ever the homemaker after her earlier indiscretions.

I don't want to return; I don't want to return to any of our homes, but despite all resistance on my part, I do return. Despite that glimmer of innate rebellion that sort of flashes on the surface of my inner well even now, despite everything, I will often find myself not lying where I know I'm meant to be, where I had rested my head. Instead, I end up somewhere else.

So here I am, awake and staring at the red and pink love heart wallpaper with my face on the soft light pillow, as it had been so many times before. A warm yellow glow from the slightly open doorway, which is otherwise dark, lights the room. My brow feels furrowed, and the wispy brown fringe she cuts is stuck to my forehead in hot perspiration.

I remember the nightmare and am breathless as if from running fast and hard. This is always confusing after the event because I'm still and quiet. Someone or something was chasing me, but my legs were so small that I could not move quickly enough to escape. They are catching up. There is a safe place; I cannot see it, but I know it. I cannot reach it, but I can feel it. Forever, the safe place is beyond my grasp.

I cry out. Sometimes, there is someone to hear; other times, there is not. This time, she comes. I am not coherent; I cannot form the concepts into language. The tears begin to roll down my hot cheeks. She is angry now. She finds some noxious-looking ointment and drags me to the nearby mauve bathroom. I try to be still and quiet again. I am afraid.

The morning is bright and sunny when I wake again, and last night's terrors are forgotten. I am dressed quickly in my short blue trousers and light cotton blouse and sit cramming breakfast cereal in my wide, toothy mouth as my mother tries hard to tame those soft brown wisps into some kind of plait, and I grimace under the tug of the brush. We have a routine, and they say it is the making of the girl, who appears outwardly happy and content. She fills her day with domestic duties and her nights with television. We see the great-grandmother who appreciates the quiet companionship and purpose of children. The grandmother rushes in and out and gifts dolls and sweets instead of time and patience. But there is balance.

Children play in the avenue after school. We bounce balls and ride bicycles while the mothers cook and wash and glance from their windows now and then to take an unconscious headcount. Our house is the kind of old-built council property with two good-sized gardens, and an outbuilding. My mother has purchased a second-hand slide for her property and a chest freezer for the outbuilding, where she keeps cheap ice pops in the summer. I slink in, thinking myself unnoticed and secrete out these cold jewels, which my mother laughingly, lovingly replaces when I am not there to see. And I love her for it, even now.

She seemed happy and relaxed at least some of the time, and maybe the voices had quieted because I don't remember her sitting and staring so much, far away in some distant place where others could not follow.

Having matured a little and experienced something of life. I think she began to wonder what the future might hold. It must have been hard to see the girls from her class go away and come back changed, doing the kinds of jobs that she could only dream of. She'd wished herself this small life when she could not envisage another. The blue wooden door, the little rose buds in the garden, a child on the swing outside. Someone else's dream. From what I remember of the conversations at the time, I think she had come to understand the meagreness of those dreams. She would huddle close with the grandmothers while they sipped their tea and glanced furtively around lest some menfolk fall lost and bewildered upon this quiet reverie as menfolk were indeed inclined to do. Like Actaeon did when Diana was bathing in the woods, but the grandmothers would prove more forgiving; after all, it was not the fault of men folk that they needed direction, and luckily, my grandmothers were not reticent when it came to providing it, discretely or otherwise. The gist of these conversations was that my mother had become lonely, and if good for nothing else, then menfolk could at least offer a little by way of companionship. It was time for her to cast the net.

Around this time, the old irritability seemed to creep back in. Only in flashes and bursts, but easily recognisable as its former self. I was in the kitchen with her once, for instance, when she threw a fist at the door of that cherished outbuilding with its yellowing second-hand freezer and that constantly evaporating supply of brightly coloured ice pops.

It was a sudden jolting sort of bang, followed by the crash and smash of glass, because her hand had gone through the window. Slippery ribbons of scarlet burst across the kitchen among shards of the old patterned window that had been on the top of the peeling door. I was glued to the spot, terror rushing through my veins.

My mother began shouting something and wrapped a tea towel around her hand. She shouted loudly, repeatedly, until I moved quickly from the house and sped off to fetch my grandmother. It was the longest journey of my life. I had never crossed a road before without another hand in mine. But we had no phone, and this was the only way. I only thought of my wonderful mother, hurt and shaking in the kitchen. She needed me now, and I would not fail her because I loved her, and she was my best friend.

Joan came later to clear up the mess, and they sat quietly talking at our yellow, chipped Formica kitchen table long into the evening, long after I had been stored in my bed to lay still and unspeaking until morning. I got the sense of some attempt at reassurance towards my mother, not me, the child, small and irrelevant. Why the anger flared in the first place is beyond the realms of recollection, but I can recall Joan telling my mother that some other version of her life was still available for the taking, that other dreams were still possible. I had come creeping down the staircase to ask for warm milk, unable to sleep for the flashes in my mind's eye: blood, glass, screeching.

There was something about a choice needing to be made, but I don't know what that choice was. My grandmother Joan told her it wasn't too late to start again. I crawled back up the stairs on my belly like a snake and slipped silently beneath the duvet. Instinctively, I knew that this was not the time to become any more of a nuisance. After all, his own desire leads man and woman. I had desires, too. I wanted to feel safe and loved.

My mother was always strangely changeable in this way. I remember once in a later time when she came at me with all her pent-up spite and venom that she seemed to store up for these special sorts of mother-daughter occasions so carefully. It was in the kitchen, too, but a different kitchen. I ran towards the back door because if I could escape in time, then she might calm down, and I could skulk back in like a night burglar when the house was quiet and sleeping. This time, though, she caught me at the door and held me tight, shouting into my face about how stupid and ugly I was, how unlovable and disgusting I was, and how no one would ever love or want me. I tried to get past, but she kicked my shins and shoved me hard so that I fell on the cold tile floor. She was strong, my mother. Built like an ox. I cried; I always cried back then. I was such a fucking sop, and I hated myself for it. One side of her lip twisted upwards because she liked it when I cried. As she shouted jeers and derision at my back, I half crawled and half ran upstairs to the room in her house that I was allowed to refer to as mine. There, I sat with my back to the door, hoping the brace would be enough to stop her from getting in. She didn't come after me this time; I think she'd got what she wanted.

I stayed in the room until morning, then tiptoed out to school to learn something. I dreaded coming home later that day, but she was bright and breezy in the kitchen as I sidled through the back door. "I've left you something on your bed," she smiled but looked away. There was a pair of new jeans sat there on the duvet.

Kept me on my toes, hating her one minute, loving her the next. I probably just cried again.

After my mother had put her fist through the window, she was a little more subdued than usual. Solemn, restrained somehow. I was too young to really understand more than the sense of her being somehow diminished. I, being of the age where I would intrinsically assume an egocentric sort of position, wondered at what I might have done to bring on this uncharacteristic moderation. I tried to please my mother but saw little change in her countenance and instead stayed mostly outside looking inwards towards the house and worrying about this new turn of events. I would sit hour after hour just looking into the house, feeling a knot of anxiety building within myself, but not understanding what it was or where it had come from. I would wait for the call indoors, but often, it would not come until long after all the other children had cleared the street and the lights were growing dim.

Soon, it was Christmas, and I tried hard to understand as family members expressed their excitement and anticipation around the event. It seems to me now that my mother continued to feel a deep and uneven insecurity about her capacity to cope alone, but at the same time was determined to prove some kind of proficiency, seeking any new opportunity available. With this inherent fervour about her person, she took me to the local shopping centre, intent on having the traditional Father Christmas polaroid that she could then display to all those around, providing further evidence of her abilities.

Well, as we drew closer in the queue, my mother became frustrated to the point of discomposure as I refused flatly to accommodate her requests, seeing the large bearded man and wanting absolutely nothing to do with him. After all, I had very little exposure to men in general, living in the matriarchal kind of unit that made up our odd little dysfunctional family. I knew that they were not wholly good and decent creatures because I had heard my mother and my grandmothers speak of it often enough.

Well, you can imagine my mother's exasperation by this point; I was proving to be all manner of difficult. She turned quite red. My mother was bustling and marching when we left the grotto, brandishing the much-fought-over picture in one hand that showed a small child with eyes red from crying. I wore a smile, though, forced from years of practice. While she was dragging me quickly away and muttering all sorts of threats about what would happen when we got home, well, our family changed irrevocably forever. Whilst my mother was marching my insubordinate self through the busy shoppers, she encountered a long-forgotten friend.

My mother was never the sort of person who liked surprises, but there are some things that leave a person quite taken aback while still remaining delighted in an unexpected sort of way. She had put those school days behind her and tried to move on with her life, so seeing such a reminder of what had been was like a bolt from the blue, and it pierced her right through that fractured, torn-up heart. She looked up towards an amicable sort of brown-haired fellow with a broad, lopsided grin and pale blue jacket. He was smiling down on her with all the warmth of a July day, and instantly, the trials of the last few months seemed like a world away. They exchanged their greetings, and she gave him her new address, all the while with me peeking hesitantly and warily from behind her legs at this new potential threat. But my mother didn't seem to notice me anymore, and she didn't seem to care at all.

Relatives have told me that I was jealous of my mother's affections, and this skewed my perspective towards the would-be stepfather. Well, I can't say for sure that this was the problem. I think it was much more besides. However, I will try hard to be as impartial as possible if such a thing as objectivity exists at all.

They had been firm friends as youngsters, orbiting in each other's trajectories since their nursery years, although having never had any more than a platonic sort of fondness for one another. It was a coincidence that had placed them in a similar circumstance, both having left school but not having moved on with the others towards a place of full independence and a world beyond the small town where they lived, Rotherham. Although a different sort of Rotherham then.

He, too, was isolated in a way, having started a business early in life, which did not leave a lot of time for socialising, or that was the common opinion of him at the time. So, he spent most of his free hours in the confines of an overly intrusive family, finding them a welcome distraction from his otherwise lonely life.

My mother and this man seemed to have an immediate understanding of one another. My grandmother later referred to them as soulmates. I don't think she was wrong.

Back when she was a teenager, my mother, living unhappily and somewhat encumbered by her parents' domestic troubles, which intruded into every aspect of her existence, well she was always sort of pensive at school, dejected looking and kind of heavy-hearted. The story goes that he would buy her a chocolate bar from the tuck shop of this old stately Grammar and take it over to where she sat in the yard, deep in the thoughts that were proving so distracting, and she would be grateful for this offering, having no lunch or money to buy it.

For the most part, this is the kind of man he was: generous and thinking mostly of others' needs because it was no secret to other families in the area that her folks were short of money, and any that did come in was spent quick on hard booze or good living, and not put into the welfare of those children, not once and not at all. My mother had been one of those kids who went without and was accustomed to the sight of domestic violence. Times have been hard in Rotherham for a while now.

When she saw him that day, it must have been like looking into the eyes of an angel, her saviour. Others, well, others often saw something else. There is no accounting for taste.

IX

LUPUS IN FABULA

(The wolf in the story)

We, as a species, have such a capacity for variation. It is
no wonder that we are so prone to disagreements. Where
one person sees warning lights and impending disaster,
another sees hope and a better tomorrow. We perceive
the world through a prism of perspective, but that vista
of possibility is changeable, based as it is upon a lifetime
of experience. My mother, for instance, saw only
opportunity when this new figure entered our lives, but
me, or my younger self, well, I remained as always
conservatively sceptical regarding the intrusion: while
she jumped in with both feet, I remained entirely
reserved and waiting on the sidelines, not even prepared
to dip a metaphorical toe into the waters.

Over the months that followed then, this new
character, Charles, or Charlie as most people called him,
well he would surface more and more, and my mother,

Cathy, began to depend and trust on him being around. She had always been the type of person to carry a sort of overly anxious concern for what other people might be thinking of her, and the burden of that divorcee status was a difficult weight to carry. She was ashamed.

'They call me a slag because of you,' she'd whisper to me when it was just the two of us, our secret girls club. I would burn with embarrassment.

'I'm sorry, Mum.' What else could I say?

'Well, just you remember, at least I stuck around.' And I was grateful because she put up with a lot from me.

When the documents of her divorce came through, she told me that she was mortified, and I saw it for myself because she stayed in her bed for more than a week. I tried hard not to be any more trouble than usual during this difficult time and would take bits of food out of the pantry when I was hungry, like the cooking chocolate she always kept in or the odd spoonful of Robinsons.

But with this new man in her life, she seemed to grow visibly in stature and from what I remember her saying, felt a little independence from the grandmothers. It was this that allowed her to walk just a little taller in the street, but the feeling always seemed a bit misplaced to me since she appeared to have just directed her reliance onto some other figure.

He would stay over at our house, Charlie, although I wasn't allowed to talk about it. He brought expensive presents, like a colour television and carefully wrapped meat. We had steak once, which I'd never seen or heard of before, and it was chewy and tough, but I had to pretend that it was nice or there would be consequences.

My mother would send me to bed early, and I would lay awake with tears rolling down my face, watching the light slowly diminish behind my red and pink love heart curtains while she giggled in the next room as the rickety old springs on her mattress squeaked loudly. I wasn't allowed to shout then if the nightmare happened. I wasn't allowed to stay with my grandmother instead. I wasn't allowed to ask questions, or talk about what I heard, or mention his visit, or complain. I didn't fully understand what was happening but had the sense enough to know that I was losing her, that she was slipping away forever. I also had the sense enough not to break the rules.

Truth be told, I felt more than a little out of sorts that this new person had come into our lives and taken away my mother's affections, and it soon became apparent that I was not the only person unhappy at the alliance. My grandmother became furious in a way that I had never before seen when she heard the news. It wasn't me that told her I wouldn't have dared, but it was a relief to have an ally nonetheless because I felt a little out of my depth in voicing those initial concerns, not being able to express myself properly and in a mature manner. So, I relied on my grandmother to do the talking but sat there in sage agreement like it was some kind of intervention.

It didn't get through, though, and from that point on, I was habitually dismissed out of the house or upstairs whenever this new visitor arrived or whenever my mother was making preparations for his visits. Applying makeup, choosing outfits, and furiously dusting. There was nothing I could do except make myself scarce.

Suddenly, I began to feel like something of an interloper on my mother's time, as she rolled her eyes skywards whenever she heard me enter a room or call out. I tried to make myself smaller, stiller, and quieter, but all the while I just became even more trouble. Anxiously, I would watch my mother closely for some indication of how I could be more pleasing, but any attempts proved fruitless.

My grandmother, meanwhile, well, she secretly fumed at the betrayal and hoped it might all blow over, reassuring me that this would be the case whenever she could. Apparently, there was some old feud between the families, in a sort of way that old families tend to feud, and the two very self-determined women that dominated these rival clans refused wholeheartedly and on grounds not easily understood by a person of my young years, to have a word said between them. So, the relationship of their children presented a difficulty in this dispute that could not go unresolved or overlooked. My mother, being in any event only still at a tender age herself, where the disapproval of an overbearing parent may actually present some quiet and consolatory satisfaction, saw no reason to fall out of sorts with what was proving to be a more than lucrative and worthwhile association. And as for Charlie, well, it is not an easy matter to understand those motivations in the early days. But what I do know is that my mother quickly concentrated all her efforts on this singular venture, with little thought or patience for the other people in her life. If he had wanted to escape, he might not have found it very easy because she had finally found what she'd been looking for, and this time, nothing was going to stand in her way.

Perhaps it is a difficult matter to explain because what I'm describing is my mother's gradual emotional

abandonment of a child that she had worked hard to bring forth. And, of course, I am hardly objective on the matter, being the said child.

I remember my mother singing, in those early days at least, smiling and laughing like she suddenly found herself free and easy in the company of that old compadre as his quick charm forced the years of hardship and constraint from her shoulders and the lines, brought early to her brow, began to ease with this new sense of shared informality. I think she felt and looked like she had been given a second chance at life.

Charlie was a natural salesman, or so they said and carried about him a sort of instinctive charisma, casual attractiveness, and an unrestrained smile that eventually wore through even the most reluctant of individuals when it was directed wholly towards them, at least. He ran his business as a family concern, and they came from all over Rotherham for that temperate patina and effortless buoyancy of his. They said he could have sold sand to the Arabs had the occasion arose, and my mother, well, she bought it hook, line and sinker.

Now seeing this improved disposition about her daughter, my grandmother became more accepting of the new relationship. It wasn't that she'd overcome the bitter quarrel that had happened so many years ago, so long ago that most people couldn't even recall the content of the argument, but rather that she could grudgingly accept the newcomer, providing he didn't bring his family along with him. With the embargo lifted, so too were so many of the rules that had been placed around his visits, and we began to spend time together, as in the three of us, me, my mother, and Charlie.

All around commented then and later at the kind of effort this new person put into a child that was some other man's to care for, and maybe this helped to ease my grandmother's temperament towards his favour. Indeed, Joan herself later said it was like he was courting me, not Cathy, in those early days, the attention and gifts that came my way. Or maybe she just saw a future where her daughter became the responsibility of some other, and she could consider her work complete. Either way, she eased off somewhat on the bitter diatribe and hoped it would sort itself out.

I must admit that I began to warm a little to his being around. As my mother busied herself with other things, it was encouraging to have someone who would be willing to play a game or get involved. I would fly around the living room watching movies on the small television set that he had bought us, playing out the scenes of my favourite characters, and this soon became central to a playground team of actors who also spent their lunchtimes saving the universe from imagined evil emperors or dark knights. Life was not too bad.

It was in this way that a new routine began to take

hold, and we started to have some positivity towards the future. But when Charlie came by one day and whispered to Cathy all the ugly words that his mother supposedly called her, 'whore', 'gold digger,' well, it was after this that a relentless sort of hopelessness began to pervade our small family home again, lingering like smoke on a thick cold fog.

However, in her eagerness and obsession to maintain this new relationship, this new hope, my mother refused flatly to acknowledge any blame, where indeed the blame should rest. Instead, she would turn her head and look at me with sudden focus, those small brown eyes tightening with a sort of reasoning as she considered all the things that were wrong in her life. Because in my mother's own troubled mind, his mother would be more accepting and not speak the way she did if I did not exist. So late at night, when we were alone, and I was sleepy, she'd tell me softly all the hateful words that were in her heart.

'It's because of you that I'm stuck here.' 'She thinks I'm a slag because of you.'

'I could have made something of my life if it weren't for you.'

Then I would lay in my shame and self-loathing and would wish and wish that there was something about me that was loveable while the tears fell down onto that soft pink pillow, and I fell slowly into a dark and troubled sleep.

Meanwhile, in my mother's mind, the voices gently tittered approvingly because blame had been attributed elsewhere as she moved quietly from room to room.

But then, within the context of all this, the context of these devastating blows to my mother's dreams, to her feelings of esteem and self-worth, to that revised kind of future that she had dared to imagine might be viable, it was here. Now, after she had tried so hard again to make a new life for us, it was at this time that I began quite un-expectedly to everyone concerned to misbehave most unacceptably. This was probably the straw that broke the camel's back.

First, it came in small bursts of tears and pleading that took my mother by surprise. After years of living in small and meagre ways, only buying what was necessary, and being careful not to be out far or long for the sake of the child, she was enjoying the new-found sense of freedom that comes with having a motorised vehicle at your disposal. She didn't drive herself but looked forward with some degree of anticipation to travelling whenever he, Charlie, the suitor, was able or available. Anywhere different can sound new and exotic when your world has become very small and local, whenever he, Charlie, the suitor, was able or available.

So, she would dress us in our finest new frocks and frills for just such an outing but found with consternation and not a small amount of quick irritation that I did not want to wear what she had carefully chosen. Well, she tried insistence, she tried bribes, she tried shouting, she tried intimidation, but all her efforts were in vain, and my tears escalated as I stood in the hall determined not to leave the house with my legs bare under the ruffled skirts. My mother would curse like a sailor at this stubborn streak; she swore that I had inherited my father's flawed personality, and with no small amount of briskness, she would pull on a pair of corduroy trousers beneath my dress, which would lead to a temporary consolation. Still, under some duress, I would finally agree to go.

Now, having little in her life in terms of outside

influence but the parents who were not always on good footing and a grandmother who was elderly and somewhat traditional in her values, my mother did what most mothers would do, and she shared her sudden woes with our small extended family.

'Spare the rod, and spoil the child' was her grandmother's sound advice, who only saw the best in her granddaughter and fully expected that she was incapable of discipline in any form. She was the apple of her eye.

So, when my mother heard the all too familiar high-pitched scream, well, she knew exactly what to do because her grandmother had told her, and so the very next weekend, I ended up leaving the house with bare legs that I so dreaded as we headed off in Charlie's old shambling blue transit van, and big red marks across them where her hand had hit. She did not spare that rod; she did not spoil that child. Depending on who was asking, of course.

Now, with my legs already red and stinging from the earlier chastisement, I reluctantly agreed to stay with this man while my mother went to buy something from somewhere, some groceries or things that mothers think of for their families. This had become our regular routine, and my mother was grateful to be rid of her charge for even a brief time. She made sure everyone knew that Charlie was very good with children and was always willing to watch me for a while.

As to what happened in that van, well I always felt unsure, uncomfortable, awkward, having no words to process or express what I was unacquainted with. There was something wrong, and in my infantile way, I had no experience or language that would form itself into thoughts coherent enough to explain this thing. I remember the feel of something, like flesh on my thigh. It was unrecognisable, unpleasant. It was wrong, and I was agitated and ashamed that I knew. I felt sick and unsettled. I was disturbed and shaking. I am disturbed. I am shaking.

Next, we were on the street, the sunlight bright and dazzling. I don't know how we got onto the street. I don't remember this.

I'd been promised an ice cream. I didn't want the ice cream. I was in the shop and he was ordering ice creams.

They were the expensive sort that came in chest freezers with pictures. We couldn't afford those kinds of ice creams, the kind in crisp wrappers with interesting textures and catchy names. I couldn't see inside the freezer. I was supposed to tell him which ice cream I wanted, but I'd never had one of these before. I didn't want any of them.

The man at the counter looked down, and Charlie rattled change in his pocket, chatting pleasantly with this new person, casually, like any other day. Suddenly, I was saying, maybe shouting, 'no' or something like it, stumbling backwards, trying to make it all go away.

I had an old leather-type purse filled with coppery discs and other treasures, and I wanted to pay for my own ice cream. He must not pay for my ice cream, and I knew that it was important. I think I had the idea that something transactional was occurring, but I didn't want to be a part of it.

I emptied my carefully accrued coppers and valuables toward the counter, but the man, well, he shook his head, and Charlie laughed heartily. It was laughable. It was laughable. They smiled down at me indulgently because

I was the joke. Then I panicked.

My breathing became shallow, and the small shop began to move upwards and outwards. I was sinking, sinking downwards, spiralling, heaving for breath, choking as the world around me became darker and more ominous, and all I saw was the laughing and the looming.

I screamed, and I must have screamed loudly, big jagged tears rolling down my face as my knees buckled downwards. The ice cream was forgotten, the smiles suddenly broken, the world fragmented, and then my mother was outside, looking inwards.

Charlie quietly explained that he'd just wanted to treat the child and asked with furtive sideways glances what was wrong with the child.

My mother was stern suddenly, angry again. I had made my mother angry. Again. I had caused a scene and made her look like a bad mother.

I tried to be good, and I tried to breathe. My mother gave her a look, the 'shut up, or pay later' look, and I tried to obey, I tried. I tried to be still and quiet, to be pleasing.

My mother went into the shop and explained

apologetically that I was spoiled and jealous. Charlie, whose smile was back in place, looked in at us with his lopsided, satisfied grin. He grinned like a wolf, did Charlie. There was a time when Charlie seemed to be the wolf in the story, maybe because he grinned and loomed like a big old wolf would.

My mother returned with an ice cream that she had bought herself. I took the ice cream. I knew that we couldn't afford the ice cream. I didn't want the ice cream. I ate the ice cream. I felt rising bile in my mouth.

I didn't want to get back into the van, but I climbed into the van. I watched on as the small shops fell into the distance and continued to eat the sweet iced dairy dripping down my best dress while I choked down the bile. My mother was furious as we headed home.

Later is a different concept for a child than it is for an adult. For an adult later is defined by the hands of the clock, by the numbers on a calendar, by the phases of the moon. Later, for a child, it is afterward.

At some time afterward, maybe days, maybe weeks, maybe months, but later, well, I just sat outside the house close to the grate where we played our small childish games, and I looked towards the house, wanting to go in but not going in. I sat there and sort of hunched down, hiding behind the rose bushes, where I wouldn't be seen, and I felt the familiar uncomfortableness in my small childlike tummy, and I rocked quietly, backward and forwards and looked on.

I could smell it myself, and it did not smell good. I knew that my mother would be outraged again, furious and vicious, but I couldn't help it. I ran all day playing with my friends in the street, afraid to go home, afraid to stay out, afraid like the greasy rough old blanket that clings to your nostrils and your mouth in the back of some old van, its coarse fibres irritating and itching your tear-streaked face, and its pollution causing you to heave as the terror rises high in your chest, but no sound comes out to mark your distress, no call for others to assist in your anguish. I was soiled, and I was sullied, and I was foul, and I knew all of this, even in my puerile way. I would never be the same again. I would never be clean again.

Another later again, my mother discovered one of

these shameful episodes, and by this time, had become so incensed with all this bad behaviour and how it might make her look to the outside world that she could barely contain her rage. She refused to take me to see a doctor, not that I requested it, but the subject was raised more as a threat and then dismissed again. Instead, she diagnosed the matter herself as a mental health problem after consulting quietly and in hushed tones with her own mother. Well, they could not have something of this nature smearing the good reputation of their family, so instead, she decided that what I needed was some good old-fashioned discipline.

So, she would throw me, as I sobbed and begged for forgiveness, into our small toilet room and slam the door shut outside once the little boy that I had been playing with from across the road had been around for the event. He sat awkwardly and still on the floor outside, not knowing what to do or say, and then never came back.

Meanwhile, my mother ranted and raved outside, and if anyone did ask questions, well, she would tell them that I was a spoilt child and a problem child and a child with mental health problems.

She called me disgusting and shameful, curled her lip back, and twisted her face in a look of pure revulsion. I was not to leave that room or open the door until I had produced, and so I would just sit there hour after hour, sobbing and sobbing, knowing full well how repugnant I was. Maybe on some unconscious level, that had been the overall intention of the act, but back then, I didn't know why it happened, only that I was bad.

Sometimes, when the phone used to ring shrilly in the background, it was as if I were released from this vacuum of yesteryear, and I would fly rapidly back to the present. I would be sitting on the stairs, rocking, crying, shocked, disoriented and reeling, breathlessly breathing small, shallow movements, with the high, persistent demands next to me. If I picked up the phone impulsively, almost compelled, then my mother would bark agitated words down the line.

X

MATERFAMILIAS

(The female head of a household)

It might have been when we learned about democracy at school that I realised how undemocratic our family life was. Democracy is a concept embedded within the principles of social equality, where generally speaking, individuals participate in the collective control of organisations or institutions, sometimes through the delegation of majority-agreed rules and laws which serve not only to maintain order but also to limit individual power, like a set of checks and balances. Sometimes, people may have a direct sort of involvement in the democratic process, while at other times, this may be more indirect, possibly involving the election of third parties to represent the interests of the whole. Or so it was explained by our eagle-eyed schoolteacher who scratched out examples on the chalky board in front of us.

This concept had a big impact on me. I think it was because when you live in the kind of society that has a democratic sort of constitutional government, at least in the sense that adults are entitled to vote on who may or may not represent their interests best, well, it becomes natural to start thinking of other associated institutions as a little democratic too. For instance, I began to wonder if the family should be a democratic unit, where each individual's opinion holds a similar degree of value to each other and where each member of that family may be afforded the same dignity and respect. Of course, the stark grey reality of my own personal experience was somewhat different, and it soon became apparent to me that my small social unit tended to be characterised by a different form of government, something altogether non-democratic; my family was inclined towards an autocratic sort of rule.

I can still remember my mother's scorn when I brought home ideas like this from the small secondary school in Rotherham that taught me and three hundred or so other disadvantaged kids skills for life and learning.

'Are you stupid or what?' was one of her favourite

rhetorics, as her face contorted with revulsion and brightened with rage. She was lying on her stomach reading the small ads when her chin turned sharply towards me. I began running, of course, because I recognised the look.

'Go on.' She shouted after me in that strange guttural voice that came with the callous laughing.

I was kept off school for a bit to teach me a lesson, 'grounded,' she called it, after some American sitcom that she liked to watch late on a Friday night. This roughly equated to a period of indefinite lockdown in the room that I was supposed to refer to as my bedroom. Just to ensure that I got the message, there would be regular and loud admonishments several times a day reiterating my worthlessness and intellectual incapacities, often through the door if I'd manage to wedge the wood in place well enough so that she couldn't get her by now substantial form through it. I would just sit in there on the coral-patterned carpet and rock and cry and think about how stupid I'd been to engage in conversation in the first place or whatever other misdemeanour had warranted this particular punishment event. She and

Charlie would sometimes loiter in the tiny landing space outside, exchanging comments about the many weaknesses and flaws in my general character loud enough so that I could hear them. She was not a negligent mother, though no, and occasionally, she would leave meals outside the door for me to collect. Things like cold mushy peas squished between two chunky pieces of thick sliced white bread. To not feed me would have been considered neglect, and she would not have anyone call her a bad mother.

So, ours was not a democratic kind of unit. Instead, we tended to rely on the heartily endorsed and enthusiastically implemented despotic regulation of one particularly power-hungry member; my mother saw herself as the female head of a household. In this way, we, as in my extended family, were and are a little peculiar, and not just in the sense of a corrosive kind of generational dysfunction that permeates each new unfortunate wave born within its confines, but also in the sense that while the family exists within a platform of democratic patriarchy, it remains quite the reverse, an autocratic matriarchy, subverting the values of a post-war, post-modern, and post-industrial kind of culture. No, my family pulls against the current and exists on the fringe; it does not move with the times.

Democracy was an attractive notion when I was growing up, but in practice, it was hierarchical regulation that characterised our household and extended family group, with a minority of individuals claiming power and control over the rest. Certainly, in our home, my mother's power remained unlimited, unbalanced, and unchecked unless by some external authority, like state, religion, or the great Lizzie-Anne. So many of the things that occurred later, the 'groundings' for instance, would never have happened when the great Lizzie-Anne was in situ. She was the true head of the household, and she ruled with an iron fist.

I wonder now what the most pertinent points about old Lizzie-Anne are and how I can share with you this pivotal figure and keep her memory alive. How will Lizzie appear on paper? Well, let me start by telling you that it was this old matriarch to whom the rigid and somewhat stiflingly unspoken and unfettered autocratic assemblage of our family life owes its demonstrably different edifice. That is one thing about Lizzie-Anne: she was essentially a tyrant. Another is that she is, or rather was, my great-grandmother. Old Lizzie-Anne was a grand sovereign of her own mini kingdom: substantial, insurmountable, invincible, or so we once thought, and although long gone from these temporal trials, she still looms larger than life in a pervasive and omniscient sort of manner. From beyond the grave, as it were.

My great-grandmother lived her life with such vigour and forcefulness that its mark remains long after, like the stain from a fine wine, which lingers stubbornly on, the only acquiescence to time detected in light and barely perceptible fading of its vitality. And they, the family that is, well, they still shudder before the strength of her towering determination manifested through the forthrightness of recollected words, a directness claimed from the entitlement of her position.

Yes, that is Lizzie-Anne, a battle-scarred penny heiress who, from the realm of remembrance alone, can still rule with the iron fist of tweed-clad tyranny because she taught her subjects well. She taught them how to fear.

Not all of us quiver at the very thought of Lizzie-

Anne's decree, though. After all, different people have different perspectives, and it is fair to say that I have nothing but adoration for the much-maligned family dictator. I can see the old girl now, like some old matron. She would peer cynically through those round plastic spectacles and roller-set brown-red curls towards the weary and submissive relative who had dragged along their baggage to be sorted and wrung. And I would sit by her knee and watch as I played with my dolls or my bricks, having long since sworn allegiance. She was my regent, ruler of this small and familiar world, smoking with calm obsession long white lung burners that the others brought as some kind of customary tribute while she doled out her judgements to the waiting throng who squirmed on the fuzzy brown acrylic of the family-sized sofa.

We all remember the wool-clad figure, with her light camel skirts and pearl embellished twin sets, but the older ones assign to that figure all their feelings of trepidation. They were subordinates attempting to placate the demands and bitter acrimony of a somewhat hostile elderly relative, grown contemptuous in her later years and antagonistic to the flippancy of youth. I only remember the comfort of her stature, the reassurance of her authority, and the indulgence of her time. And I miss that kind of surety in my life even now because Lizzie-Anne would have known just what to do. Oh, Lizzie-Anne. I loved her in a way that only a young child can love: unrestricted devotion. I loved her because she was kind.

Old Lizzie-Anne is not so lost to me yet, though, because in the quiet of the small, warm house where I live with my steadfastly ardent husband, who has quick grey eyes and a beard like the flames of a campfire in the last light of an evening sun, sometimes I listen to the ticking of the clock moving fervently onwards towards some distant later, and I can very softly, very lightly, very gradually, very gently, very unnoticeably, just slip noiselessly away. And no one will be any the wiser, least of all myself.

This is often how I find myself here, having at once returned and at the same time never left. Lining up the dominoes at Lizzie-Anne's sheepskin-clad feet, as the smoke hangs in the air like a thick London smog, and the dust dances in the sunbeams that filter through the glazed frames like tiny happy creatures in a murky pond. Every now and again, the formidable old warship, anchored by maturity to her armchair, reaches down and moves a domino on the small dark wooden footstool that is our gameboard and then breathes in deep from her white tobacco stick, flicking the ash into a nearby overflowing tray. The television rattles away with tomorrow's weather forecast, and I carefully consider my next move. This is our small and exclusive world; this is where I belong.

Lizzie-Anne was not silent on the matter of Cathy courting Charles, a member of this rival family. No, she brought down the law of her land when she heard this news, but the girl was not prepared to listen, and the old woman fully suspected that she was dancing to some other tune. Now, she knew Cathy could be obstinate, but in the end, she would toe the line, and this is what she told Joan. This is what she told herself as well when everyone else had left, and she was alone with her worries in the dusk and the smoke. It was a waiting game, and so she waited. When my mother came that day, though, well, Lizzie-Anne knew on some level that they'd lost the fight.

She sat small, always small in Lizzie-Anne's presence, with her hands clenched neatly in her lap and knees pressed together as the smoke billowed gently towards her, and Lizzie-Anne heartily drew in and blew out between tight-lipped words in hushed tones because I was in the kitchen, listening, always listening.

Joan was standing by the window looking outwards in her woolen mink-trimmed wrap that I knew had cost an arm and a leg from the department store in town. She'd brought her daughter here for the sage advice that she clearly needed because there was no talking to her. But Cathy looked up, and her lips turned into that thin pink line, and her cheeks flushed bright, and her thick brown hair brushed against her thick-rimmed glasses, and her eyes turned into those two small, round dots. So, she'd already made up her mind.

I watched all this silently, having crept into the hallway unnoticed. I gasped as my mother defiantly refused to give him up, looking small and shaky but full of staunch resolve. She got up and carefully left through the front door, passing me crouching on the patterned brown twist without a word or a look.

I saw as Lizzie-Anne blew out a long, thin line of grey smoke and looked towards Joan, saying, 'It won't last,' and as a way of response, Joan wrung her hands in worry and regret.

I, too, looked on as Cathy, my mother, stalked towards the bus stop, never looking back. My shock matched their shock, the grandmother's shock, because my mother was going against the family. We three sat there then together in our shock because what else was there to do. No one thought to ask where she might be heading or when she might be back.

Having the objectivity of age and the quiet, compassionate reasoning of one who had started life in a nursing profession, Lizzie-Anne decided to give it more time. She left the door open, so to speak so that Cathy would continue to come as she always had. It was important that she had the support of her family when all this blew over, was what Lizzie-Anne reasoned. Seeing it this way, I realise now that old Lizzie was an optimist. She believed that my mother would come back to her, and she was right in some ways.

My mother always went back to see old Lizzie-Anne, no matter what words had been said. She used to tell me that this woman had been more mother than grandmother to her, but I guess that's something I can relate to. When Joan had spent a spell in the local institution, for instance, it had fallen to Lizzie-Anne to care for Cathy, who had been nothing but a mite herself at just three and a half years old. There was no expectation of her staying with the father. I think it was just not done in those days, so it was the grandmother who stepped in and gave Cathy the kind of nurturing and stability that she hadn't known before in that short, dramatic life. She used to tell people that her mother had gone to 'gentle Jesus' as they cast their soft eyes in her direction until eventually, my great-grandmother drove the child out one day and had her mother wave from the white balcony of the grand old sanitorium at Middlewood in Sheffield. This was the only brief visit that the child was allowed, but the way my mother tells that tale, you get the impression that she was a bit disappointed to see her living.

Anyway, Joan was diagnosed with 'Nervous Troubles,' or so the story goes. Whatever on earth that means, I certainly have no idea, but she always was an anxious sort and never seemed to know fact from fiction. My mother, young Cathy, well she went back home when Joan was released, but by all accounts, it was with some reluctance because she had become accustomed to different sorts of ways, and the wrench was a hard one. She always held a special affection for her grandmother, Lizzie-Anne, and Joan never fully reclaimed the relationship. I don't know what happened in the first three years of her life, but I'm betting it was nothing good.

So, with this in mind, it was natural that Cathy should go to Lizzie-Anne for advice on her own parental struggles, and this explains how I ended up spending so much time with the older woman also how I was there to bear witness.

You see, my mother was complaining to her one day after the local infant school had brought up the delicate subject of my eating, or lack of it. There had been some problems over dinner time, resulting in an attendant sitting with me for the full hour's break to ensure that I consumed a bit of lunch. Otherwise, most of it would go into the waste as usual, so my mother was told. Now, they were well used to picky eaters, but I must have been getting a little thin because even Lizzie-Anne could see that something wasn't quite right. Of course, Cathy was furious over the matter since she figured that I had intentionally made this happen to make her look like a bad mother in the eyes of the headmaster and those others that she spoke to. She told my great-grandmother all of this and how I was a fussy, spoilt, and difficult child while I sat there on the old brown sofa feeling hot and embarrassed without being entirely sure what violation had been committed. I remember my great-grandmother looking on curiously and making little comments, which was somewhat unusual for her.

Around this time my mother's mind had become very singularly focussed, and she did not like a thought to dwell in her head too long that was not on the subject of her latest love, Charlie. So, this particular distraction was not met too favourably. She did not have the time for school visits. Nevertheless, she had attended when asked and spoken to the headmaster in low and placating tones, with her handbag on her knee and a sweet smile on her lips, telling him how she understood the child to be a little overindulged since her husband had left, and she was doing her very best to make up for that. She had tried to be patient, but obviously, she would need to try even harder. The fault was clearly her own. Oh yes, she was tired, and yes, maybe she should take a break more often. It was kind of him to think of her. After all, few did. And words to this effect.

Then she had walked me from the small village school, past the fields and the cottages, and around the corner to our home, marching quickly with that furious indignation that she had and with those small thin lips pressed tightly together so that we could have a real conversation, a nice private conversation. Because she was not going to let me ruin her good reputation. From the look on her face, I suspect the voices were muttering softly as they did of how I must be trying to sabotage her chance at happiness. I knew the expression well.

Now, hearing all about the issue at the school and

seeing how I looked a little on the thin side, Lizzie-Anne had offered to take me in a bit more, and my mother readily and gladly agreed. After all, she was trying to focus on her new life, and she didn't need me getting in the way of that. Even then, when I was only six or seven years old, she often accused me of trying to control her. I think that she was feeling the restraint that comes with motherhood.

She worked here and there for a few hours each week in one of Charlie's shops, and if there was no school to provide some form of mind, then I would be left to play in the storage areas around carpet rolls and the genuine mahogany furniture with leather inlays that were laid out waiting to be purchased.

Lonely, hungry, and bored, I would keep an eye on my mother in case she left for one of her frequent shopping trips. Charles was always very accommodating to my mother's needs. Everyone said so.

So, it was a relief to instead be spending time in the sanctuary of Lizzie-Anne, because I always felt immediately secure with one of my grandmothers close by. Cathy was also pleased to be spending some time away from the burden of motherhood, and so it worked out well for everyone.

Lizzie-Anne would smoke her long, thin cigarettes as we played dominoes on the small dark stool, and the kettle billowed merrily in the kitchen. Sometimes, we would cook together on the small Formica table, weighing out flour and sugar and dropping the mixture onto greased baking sheets for the oven. I liked to drink sweet lemonade from glass bottles that came in a small rattling van once a week, and Lizzie-Anne would put an extra teaspoon of sugar into each cup to help 'build me up.' Because as much as she might have disapproved of her granddaughter's new lifestyle, she believed that 'you don't hang your dirty laundry out in public,' and she was appalled that attention had been drawn to the family by way of the local infant's school. She'd made this very clear to my mother one day when I was safely playing outside, and my mother had made it very clear to me when we were safely home away from prying eyes. Lizzie-Anne just didn't want any more questions being asked of her family, so she did what she could to put things right.

While this was all occurring, it also started to become apparent to everyone that the much-discussed and much-berated relationship of my mother's wasn't going to end. Despite the arguments, despite the conflict, my mother did everything that she could to keep her new man, although she needn't have tried so hard, because it appeared from the outside that he was quite besotted with her too. So, when she approached the subject of a more permanent sort of situation, well, Charlie readily agreed, with, of course a few caveats of his own: he wanted us to move away. My mother didn't ask me my opinion. Of course, the thought would never have crossed her mind.

I don't know if she would have really gone through with it, though, because our family, you see, or extended family anyway, for all its autocratic, dictatorial, hierarchical, and highly dysfunctional sort of problems, were also the sort of family that stuck together. She had never lived more than a mile away from her own grandmother and had seen this woman every day of her life. As for me, well this routine had simply continued. We were the kind of people who lived in each other's pockets; we fought together, celebrated together, ate together, and died together. We had our faults, but back then, we shared our food, our homes, and our feelings. We were an enmeshed kind of family, and for all the things that people could list against us, which were numerous, well, what they couldn't say was that we didn't love one another. At least not back then.

So, to move away from the family would have been really quite unthinkable, under normal circumstances. After all, my mother relied heavily on the support of her parents and grandparents, who were collectively raising my young self, as was the tradition for some. But Charles, he was adamant, and he grinned his big lopsided toothy smile, and he spoke words in her ear as they giggled together at night. He didn't want to move into our small council-owned home in our small rural village with the mother around the corner and the Grandmother a half mile away, the only school that I had ever known, and the little hall at the bottom of the road, and the nice cul-de-sac where all the children played together in safety while the mothers watched from their windows. And my mother, well she didn't want anything but him, or maybe more of what he brought with him, it was difficult to tell back then.

Anyway, she had her arm twisted in the end, and really, it was all my fault. You see, I hadn't been feeling too well for a while, but my protestations had fallen on deaf ears. My mother thought that I was just trying to ruin her chances in life and pull the wool over her eyes, so to speak. She was having none of it. Now, Cathy, my mother, she was always the kind of person who harboured a sort of innate suspicion against the motives of others, a kind of obsessive and delusional distrust that made her automatically assume some ill intent in the actions of everyone around, to which she was almost always the central victim. She liked to take a leading role, my mother did. But, as it happened, her negligence in this matter led to my schoolteacher discovering the rash that I'd been mithering about week after week and, of course, the other more general deterioration in my health. This resulted in my very quick extraction to the nurse's office because they didn't want to risk a school-wide infection. After this, came the dreaded phone call to my mother. I was crying again, always crying, knowing full well that all manner of recriminations would rain down upon me for such a betrayal. This was going to make my mother look bad, and it was all down to me.

Now, being forced to seek medical intervention, my mother was none too happy, as you can imagine, but she did arrange an appointment with the local physician because the school had insisted upon it. So, she took out her best downtrodden, weary, devoted single mother personality for the afternoon, with, of course, corresponding apparel and facial expressions in place. This seemed to do the trick, and she left in receipt of a prescription, which would hopefully quieten me down before the end of the day. Sadly, though, it was less than effective, and a week later, the very same physician prescribed a period of incarceration at our local hospital, much to my mother's odd exuberance.

She called every close and local relative to her side, and they fussed and fretted over her numerous and very tearful breakdowns in the hospital waiting area. My grandmother, Joan, marched to and fro ward to ward, attracting the attention of anyone official looking to come to the aid of her ailing granddaughter for the appeasement of my mother's fraught nerves, and my grandfather, not one to usually become involved in such theatrics, nearly drove his tyres bald up and down the roads from our quaint little village to the post-war hospital complex day and night recovering items from various homes and houses as and when required.

Meanwhile, after some close inspection and a set of blood tests, I was diagnosed with Glandular Fever, along with Measles, Pneumonia, Impetigo, a Ventricular Septal Defect of the heart, and a most unfortunate and uncomfortable case of Desquamation. I know this only from research into my own personal medical records and, of course, the memory of my skin flaking away in a very itchy and uncomfortable manner. The family has always maintained that I had been wrongly interned after a mild case of glandular fever largely because I was a very petulant child who never wasted an opportunity to derive attention for myself, all at the cost of my poor, long-suffering mother.

At the time of the hospital internment, the ward physician came back with these diagnoses and a treatment plan, and my mother went from grieving to aggrieved so quickly that they could have recorded the change in measures of light speed. She was seething, her lips tightened quickly into that indignant thin pink line, and she became immediately adamant that I had purposefully set about to destroy her good reputation and lay waste to her happy plans. She acknowledged the Glandular Fever but fervently denied any other condition. From that day on, she told everyone that I was a fantasist and made up mystery symptoms. And they believed her, despite my only being six years old and despite any evidence to the contrary. She's good, my mother, convincing. She's convinced me a few times, and you'd think that I would know her well enough by now.

Anyway, in the hospital, being and feeling quite sickly, I had a room to myself, and my mother would come and go, popping home, as a parent might, just to have a break now and again. But one of these times, a nurse came and took me away into some kind of examination room down the corridor to administer blood tests and such. She seemed like a kindly sort and had a nice chatty manner, and me, well I wasn't really used to strange adults, or any adults, talking directly to me as such, but I answered, and it was all going fine. Truth be told, I quite enjoyed the experience. She seemed interested in me.

So, I was feeling comfortable enough, quite reassured and not at all worried, when suddenly the door burst inwards and my mother, all red-faced and furious, launched herself towards us and into the mix, sort of snatching at my arm and glaring at the nurse with those two small brown eyes. Oh, she was full of snappy retort and agitated in that bad sort of way that I had learned to dread. She shot some remarks towards the very kind lady, who was startled more than anything, but I can't remember what was said. I just remember being suddenly very afraid and bursting into tears.

My mother marched me back off down the ward and into the little room where I was staying, and this is where I got it double barrel. Because I knew, oh yes, I knew alright, yes, I had been told, that I wasn't to talk to anyone, any stranger, any person at all, without my mother there to answer for me, yes, I knew.

'You stupid girl. Don't you know what happens to children who get taken into care?'

Well, I just sat there weeping, which, of course, was the norm, but also because I was afraid and ill and hurting all over and in so much trouble. My mother she was swollen with resentment, having been put in this position, and so decided from that point on not to leave my side. And this made me cry even harder, and I wasn't sure why for a very long time.

So, they brought her a small bed from somewhere, which looked uncomfortable and tiny, and she slept there in my room. And my grandmother would send out the grandfather if anything were needed. Of course, it actually all worked out to her favour because Joan made sure to put the word out, and the neighbours, and the ladies in the shop, and the friends of the family, well, they all cooed and awed and talked about her dedication to me, the child.

'All's well that ends well,' was what old Lizzie-Anne used to say. Cathy blamed the Glandular Fever for my somewhat impoverished health and slimness while I learned never to answer questions for myself again. All in all, no harm was done.

What it was that the nurse asked, well, I could never

actually remember, possibly because of the stress relating to the incident or maybe just because I lacked the maturity to process the request. But from that day on, and right into adulthood, it was my mother who answered most questions for me while I just sat mute as the fabrications and outright lies flew and buzzed all around. I was always afraid of that little woman's wrath.

Anyway, the point of this was that the hospital visit became the catalyst for something that would change our world forever. Charlie came back having found a place that seemed just right, a house on a busy main road, miles away from where we knew, miles away from the grandmothers, from the school, from the fields that you could walk in forever, away from the horses on the corner in the paddock that would snort at you walked by to the shops, and away from all the friends who played all day in the cul-de-sac, and Sunday school where they made pancakes, and the post office that sold the sweets on high shelves in big boxes, and the green grassy garden at the back with the slide and the swing.

Charlie had found a house with a shop because Charlie was all about extending his business and making money and making a profit, because profit makes prizes, or something like that he used to say. And in front of the shop was a big busy main road with lots of potential customers to spend money in the shop, and at the back of the shop, there was somewhere for us to live and big high gates to keep the riffraff out because there could be trouble in the area at night from all the people who could not afford to spend money in the shop.

It was a place that we didn't know, and a place that didn't know us, and my mother could not have been happier because she was feeling the need for change and a fresh start where the school would not be asking any uncomfortable questions and those awkward letters from the hospital could not follow us.

This is how it came to be that one day when we were driving in my grandmother's car soon after the hospital experience, and I was sat in the back swinging my legs and looking out of the window, blowing the smoke around in small waves around me, that my mother decided on the perfect way to impart the news. We were comfortable in my grandmother's car, the three of us together, three generations all together, the older women gossiping in the front and me watching and listening in the back. But suddenly, on one of our journeys, my mother swung her head around towards me:

'Tell her then,' she insisted.

I was on the spot. What was I supposed to tell or not supposed to tell? Because if I got it wrong, there would be hell to pay. Then, it dawned on me, with some prompting from the front. I was small and reluctant, and I tried to make myself even smaller, to disappear altogether, to leave this place behind, but I was tethered somehow, as if by some unknown force, and so having no choice, I carried helplessly on.

My voice was a small and jerky voice: 'Mama, we're moving to Dinnington,' and suddenly the car filled with charge, like static electricity. The grey clouds of smoke came alive with tension, alert with anticipation.

My Mama, whom I loved, well, she turned her face slightly towards my mother and, in a small smug smile of satisfaction, as if having won some small battle that I was not really aware of, said, 'Oh, well, we're moving too.'

'What?' my mother snarled back, 'where to?' she demanded. I think she was shocked and upset that her news seemed to be smaller now, paling beside this other more surprising turn of events, and my grandmother, my precious Mama, Joan, as the others called her, she responded.

'We're moving to Hornsea,' and with that the charge ignited, and the world, my world, would never be the same again. Everything around was tainted by the aftermath of that explosion.

Now, Joan and Alf, my grandparents, they had a holiday cottage in this small seaside town on the east coast, and sometimes I would stay there too, along with my young aunt, who would laugh and sparkle in the sunshine. I loved to help my grandmother, Joan, in the garden and learn about the plants that she cared for or taste the summer berries. I was always happy in the warmth of my extended family, away from my mother and the raging, and of course, the new threat that now accompanied us everywhere. I should have asked to go with them. Maybe that would have changed things. They would not have taken me. She would never have allowed it.

MEA CULPA

I should have, could have, would have. But it is as it is.

I blink and find myself staring through the glass as the tall green trees at the side of the road speed quickly by, less dense than they had been just moments before. My husband is talking about some road sign he's seen, and the everyday mundane continues on as my stomach sinks and my head pounds and my mouth rasps dry like autumn leaves. It is the same, and it is not the same. Cigarette smoke fills my nostrils, but not the air around me. Neither I nor my husband indulge in that particular habit.

XI

ALTER EGO

(Another I)

Sometimes, it feels to me as if our lives are marked by a finite sort of impermanence that imbues everything around us with the weight of its transient changeability. We are perishable and inconstant, ephemeral, short-lived creatures, a blink on the geological landscape, with no more significance than the mayfly, buzzing frantically around, trying to fulfill a genetically pre-established life cycle before our inevitable but unpredictable demise. Too busy celebrating the perceived success of our evolutionary trailblazing, we have neglected to recognise the curse of our own intellect: an awareness of an inevitable expiration. Under the yoke of this knowledge, there is no wonder that, as a species, we have become so utterly obsessed with the concept of the ultimate. We imagine world after world as a consolation for the lack of our technological or spiritual conquest over life and pursue a desperate quest aimed at suspending the unavoidable and quite conclusive end.

I digress. What I mean to say is that transience is all around. Night becomes day, the seasons rise and fall, people come and go, and the landscape moves and sways around us. We ourselves are changed with every morsel eaten, every synaptic pathway made, with every word we read. Every cell regeneration implies an intrinsic difference on a molecular sort of scale.

Sometimes unnoticeable, in the running and the flitting, and the hubbub of everyday life, but we are distinctly dissimilar in small and sometimes indefinable ways. Day after day.

Or maybe this is just how it is for me. I am just a girl with big brown eyes and wisps of hair and fear that clings inside, all ragged and coarse, tainted and impure like the fumes from an oil spill. My mind moves this way, and my mind moves that way. Yes, I am a transient kind of creature, you see, different people know different versions of me, another I. Some know me grown, adult, and some know me young, a child. Some know me in my professional capacity, and others only in the social sense.

Now, some, well they only ever know the version of me that they have manufactured in their own minds, and this is always somewhat different to the one that others access, being mostly a projection of their own more personal expectations. They sometimes feel me out of character when I do not behave the way that they have anticipated. But regardless of how or who they think they know, what everybody's version of me has in common is a kind of dogged dependability, a kind of solid perseverance, an unwavering persistence, which some condemn as stubbornness, while others respect as tenacity. Whatever people say or do not say, I am no quitter, and this one thing remains unchanged about me in any way you look.

I will tell you this, though, and I hope that we will understand one another, when a person sits quietly at the end of their small and very personal world, watching as it slowly crumbles and collapses before their very eyes, steadily sort of absorbing the shocking and humbling realisation that all the things that they had lovingly built were no less fleeting than the delicate floating seeds of a dandelion on the summer breeze, well, let us just say that this experience can prove to be a little disconcerting. Indeed, a small seed of doubt may begin to wriggle deep into that person's mind as they begin the non-too-unsubstantial process of pondering what will follow, as they consider what the next phase of construction might look like and what sort of shape the eventual output might be. Because lives are not just handed to us, tidily and delightfully packaged by some loving hand who has thought carefully and long about just what we might like and then has shaped some marvel for us, enthralled with their own ingenuity and captivated by the anticipation of giving such a prize. No, lives are something that we must work on ourselves. They take perseverance, dedication, and no small amount of individual creativity. What is more, those that merely sit, wait, wonder, and watch, ready to follow someone else's blaze, someone else's intent, someone else's dreams, well what they live is no life at all.

This is how it came to be that the adult version of myself, all grown up and having now moved on a small way, at least from the little blue tablets that the physician was kind enough to prescribe and the six hours or more of talking therapy that the area trust was kind enough to bestow, and the squawking of the telephones which had finally and kindly now ended, this is how it was that I began to consider what to do next with what there was left of the time.

Now, having already been through the process once, well, I was all too aware of just how much toil was required to accomplish any sort of existence worth having, and I was worried because living under the heavy and oppressive blanket of stinking, oleaginous fear, well I just wasn't sure that I could cobble together the energy required for making lives, and big decisions, and purposeful sort of goals, on top of holding the weight of this encumberment, every minute of every day. But since there was no one who could be trusted to share the load, I knew that I would have to try. Trying is what I did, and trying is what eventually brought me here. But trying takes a great deal of time, and so there was much in between then and now.

So, it was in this strange and somewhat unsettling predicament that I did what some might say I do best. I decided on a course of action that would elicit a new chapter of existence, a new phase, if you will, something whereby if questions were asked, I could answer confidently and with firm self-assurance that this new situation had been one made of decisive intent to secure further and future accomplishment, and nothing, absolutely nothing, no nothing at all to do with the fear. The fear need never be raised as a subject at all, certainly not by me. And, with the familiar determination that marked my previous exploits, I launched myself headlong into a life of study and learning. After all, doing nothing was certainly not an option. I am not a do-nothing kind of person. In my experience, doing something is always better than doing nothing. Something provides a happy distraction, for one thing, a distraction from those awkward and uncomfortably intrusive flashes of abstract memory that shoehorn their way into my mind quite without invitation. I have done everything that I can think of to wipe those images clean away, including but not limited to the very literal and regular cleansing of our cosy three-bedroom suburban home. But try as I might, what I know cannot be unknown.

Now, during the time that I like to think of as my rehabilitation, the restoration of my character into a good and productive member of the community, well, during this time, I remained resolutely, and some thought quite irrationally, disconnected from the most discrepant of my relatives, the maternal family. And the feeling of isolation and separation that this engendered brought about the most profound sense of remorse and vehement dissolution. I felt completely and almost totally lost. Because having been raised in such close proximity, at least in my formative years, to be entirely divided now was indeed a quite foreign and unforeseen turn of events.

That said, I could not by any means bring myself to provoke any form of contact. Not, and this is a very pertinent point, in my opinion, not because I was too proud by any means. No, pride was never a trait to which I have felt accustomed. No, it wasn't pride. It was the fear. I was simply too afraid of their admonishment and the distant memory of those figures raging behind the door, which was all too clear now in my mind's eye. No, I could not go back, but I sorrowed and grieved at the loss of their lives in mine.

MEA CULPA

Estrangement is a difficult position to be in, especially when very suddenly, very quickly, very much overnight, you lose all of the padding from your life, all of the extra stuffing, the filling and the fluff, the extraneous comforts, the wads of cushioning, if you like. All the incessant nagging, the ringing, the moaning, the talking, the questioning, the obligating, the verbosity of life is gone, leaving only the relentless thoughts of self-doubt, self-flagellation, and self-deprecation that are sort of administered entirely unintentionally and unconsciously on behalf of those loving family members who are no longer around to administer this for themselves. I have spent much time trying to decide whether my own unvarying and unswerving critique is more or less tolerable than theirs. Judge not, lest ye be judged.

Any social situation becomes unnervingly difficult, as people will undoubtedly talk of their own families at some point in the conversation, and at this point, I will usually sink into despair and humiliation, what I like to think of as my shame place. What do you tell almost perfect strangers when the invariable pause in exchanges arises? I will usually just search around in dismay for some way to fill the void because even after all this time, I am still no longer prepared for what I lack. I no longer have a mother or grandmother. No Aunt or cousin will come to call. There are no unavoidable restrictions on family gatherings to endure. No one telephones me at the weekend or sends me birthday cards. I have no amusing anecdotes of elderly relatives to relate to a sympathetic audience. In fact, I have nothing to identify with at all. I am estranged not just from my family but from almost everyone else because of it.

If this were a competition, then they win. Every time. I am an outsider now, an outsider to not just my own small familial group, but also anyone else's. And if I confess the truth, my shame and chagrin, then I would also be confessing to that deep sense of rejection, to being unloved and unwanted, spurned by the people who are obligated above all others towards unconditional acceptance. No matter what. Suck it up, buttercup, this is what you wanted.

No, I tend not to face sharing with anyone the depths of this distress. It is easier to stay well away. Hide in plain sight. So, in disconnecting from my family, in many ways, I have disconnected from the world at large. I make excuses to explain my withdrawal. Should anyone enquire? I make those same excuses to myself. I am highly adept at denial, and this is something else that is common in all the different versions and spectrums of myself, that and loyalty. I remain always faithful to my family long beyond what is deserved and almost always to my own detriment.

The family, though, has never returned that faith in me. They did not grieve at the loss of my life in theirs. No, after I did the unthinkable that day in my pain and my haze out of desperation for the incessant ringing and squawking to cease, well, it is my understanding that the mother and the grandmother were furious towards this rebuttal of their affections. No concern or worry was extended my way, no compassion or care. Joan, now elderly, was shocked initially at such an outrage but had the full anticipation that I would soon be back, tail between legs, so to speak, and ready with apologies for this latest and most ardent insurrection. She knew me as a wayward child, a difficult child, a spoilt child, always causing problems for my mother.

So, she organised all manner of confutations to throw in my direction, sharp and decisive negations, a collection of castigations that would keep me rocking until winter. She had them neatly collated, having already aired a few of these home-weaved allegations on some of her nearest and dearest enough times to verify the authenticity of those claims in her own mind and then shaped the world to her liking. In doing so, thinking that she would subjugate me to her liking too.

Joan and my mother had created an unsteady sort of alliance after the tensions brought in by Charles had fizzled posthumously away, and it is fair to say that she had become Cathy's most ardent protector, almost making up for the time she lost when Lizzie-Anne was still alive to steal her daughter's affections. If my mother claimed to be wronged, then Joan would fight like a lioness in her defence. In those later years, anyway. And, of course, Joan had always been the sort of woman who knew how to get her own way. Unfortunately, though, her impulsive nature meant that she didn't necessarily want the things that were good for her, and so she was often left dissatisfied, disappointed, and bitterly dysphoric, living in a world of her own making. If she had been blessed with some degree of inward reflection and ability to reason, then maybe things would have been different, but as it was, she sought rationales outside of her own manipulations to explain the cause of her personal discontent, and so came into conflict with all of those around, then felt fiercely rejected when their affections buckled under the force of that well-groomed rage, projecting this anguish onto the perpetrator in the form of emotional maltreatment which was intended towards correction.

She once tried to explain to me why she behaved in the way that she did using the only terms that she herself could understand. It was an apology of sorts because she was not a woman to take ownership, and we all accepted this. She blamed her behaviour on a sort of emotional sensitivity: she said that she felt more deeply, more intensely than the rest of us, and so the world was crueller, more brutal to her than we could ever imagine. It is true that she was a passionate spirit, and when she laughed, we all laughed with her because her joy could light up a room. But when she cried, well then, we knew to leave well alone.

When I did what I did, she was at the time in her life when a person becomes wistful for the early years, having nothing much to fill the vacuum created by all those empty rooms. The things that she had collected they sparkled brightly as they caught the light, but their company was cold and quiet, and she missed the warmth of human contact but didn't know how to bring people to her. When Lizzie-Anne left this mortal plane, well, Joan had fully expected to inherit the legacy of the old matriarch's familial status and waited patiently for her dues, but the others did not pay heed as she thought was her right. It was a different time, a different dynamic, a different sort of regard, and there was no honouring, no veneration, and no quivering on the carefully selected oversized sofa as she gave her decree. She never did understand that lesson about earning respect.

So, in the absence of a literal sort of life, well, the memories came to fill the gap, as they do when a person stops making plans for their future. Perhaps she longed for the comfort of her parent's love, but I suspect it was adoration that she valued more by then.

What I remember fondest is us sitting and sipping together from china mugs in the afternoon heat. Smallish talk and flicking eyes. Rare interludes from the tension of our situation. And then the stories would come fluttering like confetti through the summer breeze as the smoke hung in clouds all around us. They would please her, the stories, and she would smile, her eyes looking beyond to something that I would never see. But then, as her attention would inevitably return to the present, so too would her belligerence and all the amity that she may have temporarily declared would be lost again, just like the gentle reminiscences to which she clung. Truthfully, it caused me some affliction to see her this way because, of course, I remembered her back then. We were never short on love, me and her, just lacking the kindness to show it. I miss her now, and that's the truth.

But, my mother, never being one to pass up on an opportunity, she saw how my grandmother's heart had turned bitter and broken with age and disappointment, and she mobilised this acidity with all the manipulation of a master because, by this point, she had really refined her art. My mother is always the longer story, and we will get there. For now, I will say that later in life, she began to take on the appearance of a person who has been slowly disintegrating, she was just never as well held together. Poor Cathy, they called her, the widow, who lived in her mother's pocket, a small kind of life, a protected kind of life, a life away from the tribulations of the outside world, away from the worry of work or strain of in-laws, obligations of friends, the authority of physicians.

'How's your poor Cathy?' They would ask my grandmother, and she would tell them all my mother's woes, starting with her ungrateful daughter, who never lifted a finger to help. May God have mercy.

Looking back, it's difficult still now to gauge how much of poor Cathy was a manufactured image and how much was down to the authentic deterioration of my mother's mind. In the family, there was a general acceptance that she was a little eccentric, but I don't remember who started the rumour or why. I, the adult me, went along with it just like the others, and we sort of cushioned her a bit against the world outside, providing some safeguarding if you like. If she needed work done to the house, for instance, then my grandmother would arrange it, pay half up front and my mother would just receive a bill for the remainder and rankle at the cost. We couldn't have poor Cathy knowing the real price, the idea would be too much for her. When she needed new clothes, I would buy something wear it once and wash it, then bag it back up and take it over. Poor Cathy couldn't afford these things, and this was my duty as a daughter. When her kitchen fell into a state of disrepair, it was my Aunt's husband who footed the bill because poor Cathy could not stretch to such indulgences. No, poor Cathy needed sheltering from reality, and when the full actuality of why she needed sheltering finally became apparent against the frenzied protestations of Joan, that is when the careful construct that was our little family detonated with the ferocity of an atomic warhead. Nothing but ash and devastation for miles. Because the illusion or delusion surrounding poor Cathy was actually the thing that held us all together. Who knew?

I don't think that I truly understood what a hard time it would be for my mother, for the girl that was Cathy, or poor Cathy, or adult Cathy, or any version of Cathy when I finally walked away. She was not a person given to trust easily but she had trusted that I would always be a part of her life. Now, her mother, my grandmother Joan, well she did not help the matter, talking as she did. But they both agreed that I was detrimental and maybe a little bit dangerous to their cause and that they were, of course, in no way to blame.

So, they mitigated any potential threat to their tiny handmade universe by talking freely and openly to all that would listen about all manner of woeful things, attributing them in earnest to the runaway so as to fully negate themselves from any guilt regarding the matter and in addition systematically destroying any ounce of credibility that I may hold, should I attempt a counterattack. Reality, of course, is neither here nor there for these two.

Cathy struggled to recollect almost anything anyway, whether that be me, her telephone, her telephone bill, or what had happened in much of her life, and she relied on Joan to fill in the gaps, who supplied it happily from her own interpretations of what Cathy may have told her way back when adding a little twist here and there when it seemed appropriate and for her own motivations. It was a social memory in practice.

In this way, Joan provided her daughter with relevant communications and updates, like who to trust and who not to trust, and Cathy listened closely and acted accordingly. Sometimes she would repeat the information to other members of the family, and this would give Joan's information a sort of credibility. Finally, then in these later years, Joan had become a very important figure in Cathy's life, at least as important as the voices whom she also relied on with increasing impartiality.

Some of us exist in the most significant moments of our lives, endlessly. Now, this doesn't mean that we don't learn and develop, that we don't evolve and mature in that organic sort of way that people have a habit of doing emotionally, physically, and intellectually. No, what I mean by this is that a kind of version of ourselves seems to continue on forever in every notable instant of our lives, like an opaque shadow of a former self, a wispy rendering that remains forever in the immediate, captured like a butterfly in a jar, fluttering senselessly at the sides of the dome, unable to liberate itself, unable to just fly away.

I always had the impression that my grandmother, my mother's mother Joan, well that she was trapped in the instant of her earlier breakdown, in the moment of abandonment of parental responsibility. However blameless she may have been for this, and for Cathy's own difficulties, it always seemed to me that Joan was driven mostly out of guilt and unable to see clearly what was right in front of her nose.

In moments of quiet deliberation and private speculation sat together in the afternoon heat, she would access the series of editions that made up her earlier life, revisiting, reinterpreting, and re-understanding. Almost flicking through the figurative former like a well-organised lever arch file, examining the variants, the conspicuous, the individuals, and then editing to assuage her culpability against the context of the wider accusatory whole.

Joan was a woman conquered by her own demons, misplaced within the stratigraphy of a life lived. She was a woman lost.

XII

NEMO MALUS FELIX

(Peace visits not the guilty mind)

Time passed and years passed, and weeks and moments passed from the drama of the night sat kneeling behind the door with the fear for the company and, the blue flashing lights and the telephone shrilling and the numbers changing and all of the life-altering events that occurred so quickly and spontaneously and shockingly and in some cases, regretfully because time waits for no man and no woman either.

With this passing of time, I began to understand somehow that it was not what had happened that proved to be most difficult, not the door and the noises and the bangs and the unexplained, but rather the remembering of what had been. That is, the sudden and vivid, disturbing recollection of images that had arrived one evening on a cold winter night, packaged all neatly with the additional heart-pounding shock of unwelcome intruders in what I had previously thought of as my refuge, my reserve but above all, my home.

Despite this lapse in measured minutes, hours, days, weeks, and months, despite this continual progress, as it were, in the succession of other living things, in the succession of the seasons, in the succession generally all around, well, I remained in many ways no further forward than I had ever been, still sort of trapped within the moment. I remember the flashes of vexation back then that came in the form of a kind of exasperated sort of aggravation, but you see, I was so completely confused and bewildered, so entirely perplexed, that it was almost impossible to process any of these unbidden thoughts properly. All I really wanted was for them to settle nice and deep inside again, like the way that someone might diligently weigh down their darkness in an old trunk at the bottom of a cold and forbidding ocean, letting it sink gently and slowly into the unfathomable blue-grey hue and gaping sediments. Imagine how that person would feel if some chance wave washed that barnacle-encrusted crate right back up onto the sands again. It felt like there was no getting shot of it.

So, with those recollections free and roaming around, rattling their chains occasionally for attention, demanding all sorts of observation and recognition, I had an awful lot to consider. I mean, really, it's not like I hadn't thought about these things before sometimes when they came floating up to the surface, but you see, back from being as small and as young and as naïve as I can honestly remember, well the people that I naturally trusted most in the world, those that I had counted on for my very survival, my primary caregivers if you like, well they had told me repeatedly again and again and again and again, that I was the most loved, the most over-indulged, the most fortunate child of all children, and that I had the best mother, the most devoted mother, the most self-sacrificing mother of all mothers, and that I had been the worst daughter, the most obnoxious daughter, the most poorly behaved daughter of all daughters, and had put that mother, that dutiful wonderful kind and caring mother and all of my compassionate and much superior relatives, through all manner of awfulness, being as I was. An all-around bad apple. Peace visits not the guilty mind. Oh, for a moment of peace.

For the longest time, I believed them. Maybe I still believe them now. Maybe this is because I believe in my family, or maybe this is because I don't believe in myself, but whatever the reason, believing that I was just sort of inherently substandard and thankless was most certainly better than the alternative. It is a little white lie that I clung to. My mother used to tell me that little white lies were okay.

'No, now you're bullying me, and I won't have it. It is perfectly okay to tell little white lies if it saves someone from getting hurt,' she would retort indignantly whenever I tried to challenge her on this. Then call my grandmother quickly and tell her that I had shouted again. There was little point in denying it because everyone knew that my mother was beyond reproach. And I thought that these little white lies did indeed prevent me from being hurt. Losing it all. Losing them all.

Maybe I should have been a rock climber, because I held onto that ledge for so long that my hand cramps just thinking about it. But there was always this sneaky kind of insidious sort of creepy little incompatibility problem that kept weighing me down, whispering all of these little confusing and undermining kinds of doubts. Memories. Annoying little memories that reproached the carefully woven stories that they told me and other people. Did they think I wouldn't recognise the discrepancies, the resounding clashes? Did they think that saying a thing would make it so? It is an insult, the divergence, when I think on it now, when it arises. I can never quite resolve the conflict; I am caught between love and hate.

Pack it down deep inside. Don't think. Because the thinking makes my head spin and my stomach feel all nauseous, like the churning inside an automatic, fully electronic washing machine doing fourteen hundred revolutions per minute. But it always finds a small gap to wriggle through. Catches me unawares.

Sometimes, for instance, it comes when I'm sitting on the big, soft, comfy sofa in our nice little house, with my big, soft, comfy ursine-like husband watching some late-night drama, some television composition, some overly dramatic theatrics on the forty-eight-inch LCD mean, lean, black sheen wide screen that he was encouraged to purchase with claims of glittering generality and bandwagon endorsements. And I'm not really watching, but I'm watching him watch. Because he likes to watch, and I like him doing something that he likes to do. Then, it can creep in. Because my mind is not busy enough, and so a tiny little gap must present itself, and there is the wriggling or the slithering and then, bam.

'You're always busy doing something, aren't you?' they'll say to me. 'I like to keep busy.'

My husband is one of those quiet, noble people who live their lives with an unspoken quality of virtue surrounding them. He is a man of quality my husband, "a gentleman of integrity," I think the quote goes. Men like my husband deserve better than a passing mention, to be a supporting character in someone else's story, but on the other hand, my husband, being as he is, righteous and fair, well, he should play no part in what this is. He has no head for horrible things, and he was never made that way. At the same time, my head has seen all manner of horror. On the outside, of course, I am all manners. Decorum and civility are what people see. But inside, it rages still, gnashing, clawing, biting, grating disparity.

Why me? I wail. All self-pity. I have no grace, at least not here on the inside.

It comes as a relief sometimes to ever so quietly, ever so lightly, ever so carefully, just slip away and leave instead a wispy, almost ethereal version of myself to flap fruitlessly and hopelessly within the almost insubstantially thin dome of juncture that represents this instance in time, while I instead flap fruitlessly and hopelessly against another. Sometimes, I actually just want to go home. Which home?

This rather flimsy and immaterial version of myself will be sitting and watching and generally filling in for the more significant, substantive whole, which may be sitting and watching somewhere quite removed in both space and time, perhaps on this occasion up to its short legs in stagnant water trying to catch a rather evasive sort of unperturbed snail, or possibly having escaped over the wall to wander in the wild burnt grasses of summer towards the small football ground and beyond to see the interesting sorts of birds roosting in the trees behind the tiny stadium. Sometimes, it is not such a bad day to be caught up in.

Since the move to the place that they called Dinnington, well, life had changed quite consequentially. For one thing, we had gained an addition to our small family, a father figure in the form of this man Charles, the wolf in our story, who had purchased the property for us all to live in and who had become quite significant in my mother's life. The significant other.

The house had a small shop on the front, which my mother ran as a growing concern, selling merchandise from his business and thus making a little extra money in terms of part-time wages and whatever on the side, meaning that we were no longer dependent on any form of state welfare. It was a fairly large house or home on the back of the shop, intimidatingly so to someone of my small stature, with three good-sized bedrooms, two good-sized bathrooms, one for each floor, and even a small en-suite in the main bedroom, which my mother never stopped talking about. She held her head a little higher these days when walking along those concrete streets and paths up and down the main road outside and about. She seemed a little taller, in everyone's opinion.

MEA CULPA

My grandparents and beloved great-grandmother had deserted like rats on a sinking ship, moving swiftly away to that small coastal town in the East and leaving us quite cut off from the support of our extended family, except, of course, by telephone. This is hardly the same thing for a young child who speaks not in words and small talk but in the expressive language of gesture and feelings. I was bereft of their familiarity and knew Charles to be the culprit for their recent departure because my grandmother had told me so. He had swooped in and broken our family up, and I hated him for it like only the oppressed can hate. It was a dedicated sort of malice. Of course, all this bad will did was increase my apprehension about the move, but what reasoned argument could I put forth against it, being as I was just a child, and these matters, like where we were to live or who we were to live with, these were my mother's business, not mine. 'Children should be seen and not heard' was my mother's mantra, and when I felt the disparity of some injustice brought against me, then 'I'm your mother. I'm not here to be liked,' which was often just as well.

These philosophies came into force more so now in this new place, as she tried hard to balance her first real adult relationship with the commitments of running that small shop with the idyllic little leaden bay windows out front and, of course, our family home. I tried to make myself motionless and quiet, or better still, be out of the house altogether and as far away as possible on my two very short legs. Because the seeing part largely only came into practice when we had visitors or indeed became them. This was when a new set of rules came into force with the explicit intention of ensuring that she did not 'look like a bad mother.' Otherwise, I was meant to be outside or upstairs, somewhere else and out of the way, the location of which could be weather or mood dependent, much like an object that you might store away until you had a need for it. And with the family so far away, it was rare that she did have need.

My grandmother Joan, she used to tell everyone that her daughter Cathy never did a thing without the child, that I went everywhere with them, and that the couple made the perfect parents. This caused one of those loud, annoying discrepancies in my mind because I remember spending so much time alone, or at least away from them, and sometimes this included sitting quietly in the dark, afraid and anxious, waiting for them to come home, hoping that they would come home, and being very careful not to make a sound in case there was trouble when they did get home.

But on a good sort of day when the weather was bright, then I would play for hours outside in the garden or climb the wall at the back and lose myself in the long grasses and the football grounds. I missed my friends from the nice, quiet cul-de-sac but had grown accustomed to spending time outdoors, and soon found a few new friendships that helped with the loss. So, I would wander around trying to find their homes in the nearby rows of identical red brick houses, which had few identifying features.

Unlike other families, we did not adhere to the regimen of deliberately organised meals and routines, and this left me mostly free and breezy. When hunger did overcome the pleasure of play then I would hurry back home and scurry through the back door, climbing the stool that had been provided for just such a purpose, and mix milk with chocolate powder into a tasty shake. It was not the same as the ones in the hospital that had been mixed from packets into large icy jugs, but something like, and it gave a sense of nourishment. If I was feeling sly, or the regular ingredients had not been provided, then I would sneak a few precious spoonsful of gravy granules from a low cupboard, but not so many that anyone would notice. My mother was busy, and I was not to bother her.

There was no grandmother living locally to lend a hand. Things had changed significantly. But if one should appear, then my mother would produce some elaborate spread at the table, and I would sit there prim and proper with my cutlery because the idea was to pretend that we ate like this every day and mostly at the same time. They would leave satisfied that all was well, and after their departure, the pots would sit on the side for a week or more, obscuring my easy access to the chocolate powder unless Charlie took it upon himself to wash them. He was good like that, tidy.

Dinnington was one of those satellite towns that sort of revolved around nearby larger settlements, cities and such things. It wasn't really a village, but still small enough so that it only had one high street, and this was where we were situated, in a large semi-detached property that extended onto the back and had tall wooden gates that opened onto a rugged scrubland which acted as access to the property. The garden at the back was a pleasant one, though, not because my mother or indeed Charles had any patience towards such things, but rather because this was the condition in which the property had been purchased, and we were not there long enough for it to fall into disrepair. I remember the high dreams and future plans that they discussed for the large outbuilding, but like most of their schemes, this never came to fruition.

Now, unlike the place where we had lived in before, this district was more urbanised. Instead of the fields and hedgerows and horses to feed and stroke on the way home from school, well, instead of these things, there were fast cars, and miners' strikes, and big brick buildings, and row on row of chimneys and those kinds of houses that all line up in neat sorts of patterns, and are very close together, and are marked by the lack of anything green anywhere outside or in-between.

Yes, this was a very different sort of place. Whereas at my previous small and rural school, I had known my teachers and my headmaster, and they had known me and all of the small and happy bright children who would play together in the yard at lunchtime, here the conditions were quite dissimilar. The school was very large and very foreboding, and the sirs would beat the children who misbehaved with a slipper or ruler and look ominously on towards any child who did not perform in the correct and appropriate manner. Classes were larger, and the children were more boisterous. No one wanted to play the silly schoolyard games, and instead, they spoke a language that I was unsure of and had only heard from my mother when she spoke in anger when things were going to get ugly.

There was no one who would notice if I ate or didn't eat and report back with meaningful questions to my slightly embarrassed mother, who frankly was quite grateful to be given this fresh new start. Yes, this was definitely a very different sort of place.

Cathy, well, she was very happy with our new

situation. She carefully and mindfully decorated each new room, selecting paints and colours, furniture and carpets, now, of course, having the means to do so, what with Charles' business and her own small piece of the pie. My bedroom was the largest room on the first floor and was carefully chosen given that the noise from the road would not be suitable for guests or for the happy couple, so it was little use for anything else. Well, my mother spent days studiously painting small pink and blue rainbows on the walls, which everyone commented on, especially after she had pointed them out.

'Oh, how lucky the child is,' they said, and well, Cathy couldn't help herself but agree because she wished that her own mother had been so diligent and mindful of her needs.

You see, although she was young, my mother had a very firm view of how to parent a child, and while she invited input from her very close relatives on occasion, she considered herself above the advice of almost everyone else. Her philosophy was mainly based around considering what she perceived her own mother to have done and then trying very, very hard to do something quite different. Now, unfortunately, this was not an exact sort of science since Cathy's issues with Joan remained unresolved throughout her life, and so her own behaviour was undeniably impacted by those early experiences. In addition, her perceptions were always somewhat flawed by a sort of misapprehension that she tended to generate in regard to most or almost all situations.

She had a kind of internal battle raging, a kind of love/hate alliance with Joan. While for the most part, she exhibited a sort of intense animosity towards her, taking the form of antagonistic come-backs and scandalous tittle-tattle, at the same time, in her later years at least, she appeared to be almost entirely dependent on this figure, her ability to survive almost seeming completely contingent on her mother, a matter which in itself became a source of further frustration and detestation. It was a highly dysfunctional sort of relationship, but even with the distance between them, Cathy relied almost fully on her family for support, which, after the demise of Lizzie-Anne, became centred very much on her mother, Joan.

MEA CULPA

Now, I think it is fair to say that my mother had been struggling with me and what she considered to be increasingly erratic and unacceptable behaviour, but things began to worsen with our new living arrangements, to the point where she became both incensed by and perplexed with what she deemed as entirely unfavourable conduct.

Cathy always saw herself as the kind of mother who coddled and pampered an ungrateful daughter and was not shy in letting others know about it. She felt herself to be the victim of our relationship, which would make me a sort of assailant because she had a tendency to think in polarities. Anyway, her sentiments were usually supported by Joan, who sympathised with her predicament, having not really enjoyed motherhood herself. I think Lizzie-Anne just worked to placate her, and so my mother would tend to sway towards the opinion that best pleased her out of the two in any given situation.

All of these women neglected or fully refused to consider the recent change as having an impact and considered only how the behaviour may affect my mother rather than reflecting on what this might indicate in me. Neither did it occur to anyone to seek advice from outside of the family, such as a child services professional, and certainly not a doctor, after what had previously been said behind closed doors in the hospital. They would do nothing that could negatively impact their reputation.

Meanwhile, what had begun in our former home continued, and I began more regularly now to soil myself, my underwear, sometimes my clothing, in a manner that was most embarrassing for my mother, and furthermore, entirely unresolvable despite the shouting, threats, violence, terror, and all manner of raging around the place. She was at a loss as to why this show of discipline proved so unsuccessful and continued to up the ante with each new round.

My mother was infuriated by it and felt very fortunate indeed that her new life partner was so tolerant.

'You're disgusting,' she would spit at me, her face all red with rage, 'what do you think Charlie must think of you? You're lucky that he's sticking around. Adam doesn't want to know, does he?' But I didn't feel lucky at all.

My mother had taken the precaution of not registering me with a local health practitioner after we had quickly moved, given the spurious comments of the last one, and seeking out the help of a physician was unthinkable for obvious reasons. This predicament caused her worry that others should discover the situation, and she resented the fact that I seemed intent on making her look like a bad mother wherever we went, being still more than a little disgruntled over the remarks made in the hospital and having decided that the matrons there were looking down on her youth and divorcee status. Yes, the world at large was trying to undermine her maternal prowess, and it wouldn't be the last time something of this nature happened.

In the end, she put the matter down to attention-seeking, and she was having none of it. So instead, she stepped up the berating and switched that look of scorn and twisted derision towards me whenever we were alone, making it understood that she considered me to be repulsive and repellent. All signs of affection were retracted both in private and publicly, and never once did my mother ever voluntarily put her arms around me or tell me that she loved me from that day to this. Her revulsion was quite genuine.

I know amidst all this worry and upset, my mother was grateful to have Charlie by her side, who would stand behind her in a motivating capacity, smirking towards me and generally having her back. You know what they say, two's company, but three is a crowd, and after a round of what she liked to describe as 'discipline' back then when I would be left crumpled and sobbing upstairs, then they would go down to the atmospheric coal fire downstairs and congratulate each other on a job well done. Sometimes, I could hear them simpering pleasurably together, seemingly in high spirits. So, where she may have once had misgivings regarding her approach to the matter, now she had someone who actively encouraged it. They were in this together.

I never did warm to Charlie, even though my mother tried to force the relationship, and this only presented a further source of continual frustration to Cathy, who often accused me of being a 'spoiled brat' and 'ruining her chance at happiness.'

My mother, and everyone else, in fact, they just couldn't imagine what I had against this kind and generous man and began to suspect that I was jealous of this newcomer, who monopolised so much of my mother's time. This presented some new material for the daily conversations over the telephone with the grandmothers, of course, and the frequent admonishments of myself when no one else could hear. But what she didn't seem to comprehend was that I saw something else in him, something that she seemed to accept with an easy acquiescence.

So, we all continued in this awkward manner, with my problematic behaviour continuing and my mother's dissatisfaction growing. It was here, like this, under these circumstances, that I first started to experience a highly uncomfortable, highly undesirable sort of frustration of my own. It was anger, I think. Dark and ugly, dank and seething. A kind of deep thwarted vexation that my mother must have been familiar with. I need you to know that I sympathise with her. With Cathy. I want you to sympathise with her too. It's not always easy to get that across. The sympathy.

To feel such outrage, such exasperation was some new kind of torment for me. It was a suffering that I could not describe to carry that rage around inside, all welling up inside, dark and thirsty for some outlet. You see, my mother has had that rage all her life, and I managed to ditch the stinking mess somewhere along the way, in some forgotten dump or dive. How the hell she ever lived with it, I will never know. Well, I guess I do. She poured it all out towards me and others. I can't take all the credit. Of course, when I felt the burden of discontent, well I responded in kind, communicating these new and intangible feelings the only way I knew how. Give, and it shall be given unto you.

When my mother or one of the grandmothers, or maybe the aunt, would tell me what an abominable kind of child I was, how hard I made life for my mother, and how badly I had behaved. Well, I knew that they were right because, in truth, I did behave badly, and I am ashamed still now to admit it. But I will try at least to make my confession here in an account that is unlikely to be read by anyone else but me.

We were poor, my mother and me, poor as church

mice, she used to say. Because of this, I was raised with a healthy respect for money. We had little of it and watched where every penny went. If I received the odd copper or note for birthdays and such, then I stored it safely in an old oversized brown leather clip-top purse. Sometimes, I would take the purse out of its hiding place and count the money as a sort of precaution against anxiety. Always, the purse would be put back safely because it was important to hide such things against the threat of those outside who wanted to take what little we had. Money wasn't easy to come by.

When my mother insisted that I lend Charlie the notes I had stored, well I was naturally reluctant, despite assurances that the precious savings would be restored in full. But I did as I was told because, at the end of the day, I was the child, and they were the adults. This was made quite clear. I was confused, though. It was against the rules.

Anyway, afterwards was when the real trouble started, because I asked for the money back. I still swear that this was the agreement we made, but my mother maintained, with Charlie in his now very familiar supporting role, that I was not owed any return. After all, he was keeping a roof over my head.

This is the first time that I remember the burn. Injustice. I was furious. Anger like I'd never known raged through my body like wildfire. I was bewildered, I cried, oh did I cry. I screamed, banged, stomped, thumped, and reached a point of no return because I could no longer live under these intolerable circumstances.

Meanwhile, my mother and Charlie, the new alliance, lay downstairs in the living room on the soft cream leather sofas that she had carefully chosen and laughed and mocked and teased and sang songs together as I threw my clothes and treasures to the bottom of the staircase, then stuffed them into carrier bags as big wet salty tears ran freely down my face and into my nightshirt. I was leaving, I didn't know where, I didn't know how, but I had to get away. As they continued to jeer, I began to panic. I couldn't breathe, and my face was red, my eyes bloodshot. My pigtails sticking to big red, wet cheeks. Finally, my mother, with growing concern that some neighbour might overhear this unprovoked outburst, rose from the sofa to settle me down:

'I'll give you something to really cry about in a minute,' she threatened, smirking back towards Charles for approval as he beamed back affectionately. It wouldn't be the last time that I tried to run with ever-varying degrees of success. Afterward, my grandmother would sometimes sit on the phone and give me a talking to, as my mother looked on with a self-satisfied smug smile, and I sat there all red and shamefaced as my many faults were recounted back to me through the receiver. God, I wanted to wipe that fucking smile off her face because I hated the bitch, but at the same time, I hated myself even more. She did a real number on me. My mother did.

Truth be told, she did a real number on Charlie, too, although he didn't work that out until much later when it was all too late. You see, Charlie was the kind of man who liked to pull the legs off spiders one by one and watch them struggle. It was just in his nature. As for my mother, well, she had been the kind of girl who had melted jelly babies on a small tin lid and then force-fed them to her weeping younger sister just to make her cry.

While my mother's character might have been

somewhat malleable, in these early years, Charlie was putty in her hands. My grandmother used to say that they were meant for one another, and I think she was probably right. But Charlie was somewhat different to my mother in that he was capable of remorse. We'll get to that later, all in good time.

XIII

FAMILIA SUPRA OMNIA

(Family above everything)

My family is always a little difficult to understand and even more difficult to explain. You see, they are the kind of people who maintain very separate, very divided, and very different public and private lives, with two somewhat interdependent sets of unspecified and unexpressed rules relating to each of these communal and personal identities. Transgressing those rules associated with public life now is simply unforgivable because building, maintaining, and above all, circulating a positive outward reputation for both the family and the primary individuals within it, well, that is of the utmost importance. Extensive energies and resources are poured into this pursuit.

From a very early age, I learned what was acceptable and what was not, who I could trust and who I could not, much like any other child. But for me, anyone outside of my immediate maternal family would always fall into the second category. This included Charles.

Now, my mother, well, as in all matters relating to public appearance, she was nothing if not conscientious in her training of what she considered to be a very unpredictable and wayward daughter. Yes, life dealt my mother many blows and misfortunes, but by far, the biggest disappointment would always be thought of as my good self. We were stuck with one another because while she may have threatened regularly enough to have me 'placed into care,' impropriety always prevented her from relinquishing herself of the burden. So, we fumbled along together as best we could, she doing her best to coach me by way of an incessant kind of negative rhetoric about the world and the people in it, and me developing a kind of continuous internal mono dialogue of beratement much like white noise that would continue for the rest of my life because she would not always be around to administer this scolding for herself.

This perpetual pedagogy comes in useful, though, at times, and certainly did during my early years when it could help me to avoid causing her further troubles. I remember, for instance, that at the school in Dinnington, extracurricular activities were available in the form of guitar lessons, much to the delight of my mother. Now, by way of some explanation, as a child and teenager, she had quite fancied herself a singer and fully expected to achieve some kind of stardom had it not been for my untimely arrival. My mother told me quite frequently about her brilliance not only in music but in many different subjects while hissing shiftily in the kitchen about how she was an 'underachiever' with her hands tightly squeezing my shoulders.

Although it was never explicitly communicated, I always felt obliged to try and succeed at any endeavour that my mother approved of, and she would bask in the light of that success, seeing it as a reflection of her own potential and worth. Any achievement that she did not approve of would feel the full weight of her personal contempt and scorn until it diminished into obscurity or, worse still, ignominy.

Well, she signed me up for guitar class before I even knew what the instrument was, so it came as a bit of a surprise. Then, of course, she rushed out to purchase a new Spanish six-string acoustic made of soft, light cypress and proudly brought this along to the first lesson, only to be told that I was not able to handle the full-size version at the tender age of seven. I still remember the face on her because the guitar teacher was a bit forbidding, and it seemed like my mother might have met her match. As you can imagine, she was not overly impressed that this little venture had cost her money but rushed out a second time and purchased an additional smaller version, and such was her enthusiasm for this new pursuit. Already, I was beginning to feel the pressure.

So, sat with the oversized guitar on my knee at home, I would try out the few chords that we had learned in the classroom, and my mother would sing along gaily in her child-like voice, which she reserved for such events. Everyone, including Charlie, I think, felt the tension at this point. But we would all feel a little light of spirit in the evenings because my mother seemed to retain this favourable and infantile personality for some time afterward. Trust me, it was better than some of the others.

This nearly came to an abrupt end one day though, because halfway through our weekly lesson, the sir suddenly became angered. I was not performing as well as he expected, honestly having no skill at all for a musical instrument, but also maybe because I was only allowed to use the large adult-sized guitar at home, and it was difficult now to place my fingers correctly on this smaller model. Perhaps I had just frittered away the practice time instead? I don't know. I was seven. But anyway, this sir told me that I was not good enough and to pack up my things and leave.

Well, I knew exactly what my mother would say because I could hear her voice in my head already, going on like it did almost incessantly. She had spent good money on these guitars, and I would pay for my mistake. I was absolutely panic-stricken. There was no way that I could go home and tell her what had happened. I broke down immediately into inconsolable sobbing and left the room running, leaving behind all the music sheets and bags. Outside in the big hall where we had assembly and games, I wept freely, and sir came out all shocked and apologetic. He had been hasty and regretted the action but insisted that I practice more frequently from this point forward, and on agreeing to this condition, I was admitted back into the guitar class and my mother need never know. She never found out how close I came to failing her that day, and fortunately, the guitar class was not an issue for much longer.

It's a strange experience to write down these recollections from our private family time. I feel self-conscious. Perhaps I'm just ungrateful. It's not like I grew up in some war-torn country. It could be so much worse. And it wasn't easy. I can make peace with that. I was not an easy child. Other things are not so easy to make my peace with.

There are memories. Unpleasant, randomised flashes of memory. More images than memories. Incoherent. Not words. Feelings. I'm there, but then I'm not there. Present and not present. Bad memories. I don't like it. I want it to stop. They make me feel uncomfortable and disoriented, sort of sick and shameful, like a filthy old disused rag might feel when it's left out in the rain and the night for a few weeks because it's so dirty and worthless that you just step over it, instead of going ahead and throwing it away with the rest of the trash. Assuming, of course, that filthy old rags had any emotional capacity. Disturbed, unsettled. Am I making any sense?

I see the trench coat. She's laughing. Does that mean we're laughing? He's there. We're not laughing anymore. It's all odd and perturbingly fragmented, and it doesn't have that associated narrative that memories have. We didn't talk about it. In fact, the idea was to not talk about it. I remember a bit of a weird conversation about it. Like the background that normal memories come with. I don't know how to assign chronological conditions to them or some kind of plot. Stories need plots, don't they?

Some of the moments have a time associated with them, though they have padding. Like a six-week period, in fact, that specific. Because Charlie had been diagnosed with some form of inner ear infection and wasn't able to drive. Housebound. A word I remember. My mother said the word on the telephone again and again.

Coincidentally, this was our first summer living in the house at Dinnington and my first summer holiday from my new school. If my memory serves me well, I think it turned into our only summer there, too. Memory rarely serves me well.

It was a most inconvenient time for being housebound, but after some discussion, he and my mother formed a plan, and she was very pleased about it. Maybe she had formed the plan, but he was too ill and worn to argue. My mother has a way of wearing people down. Anyway, it was decided that she would go on the bus every day to take care of his business in town, and I would be left in Charlie's care. You can imagine my reluctance concerning the arrangements, given that, as I have previously stressed, I never did warm to the man. In fairness, though, he was often better to be around than my mother.

Anyway, off she went to perform this new role, with a very cheery disposition indeed, waving her family goodbye, leaving me to find ways in which to amuse myself each morning, which I never found too difficult.

I don't think it was a huge concern because, at seven years old, I was already relatively independent. Children are different now, or maybe I was different then. I'm not sure. But I was well used to being alone and fending for myself and didn't really need to be told not to stick my finger in a plug socket or to take care walking across the road. I could run my own bath, dress and undress, put myself to bed, and make my own milkshake or cereal. If we ran out of milk, then I could bob to the shops for more. Mine was a self-sufficient sort of life.

This was a good thing because Charles spent a lot of his time that summer lying on the sofa, and I just came and went. I would visit my young friends whose mothers were always good for a sandwich or a bag of crisps while still bobbing back every now and again to check on Charlie as my mother had required, providing what provisions I was able to muster, given the problem of manual dexterity. Sometimes, my mother might have given me a list of household chores to accomplish, which could include cleaning the bathrooms, dusting, and generally tidying the place up a little. I did my best and sometimes roped in a friend to help, which made the work more fun.

For the most part, Charles ignored me, sleeping in an old brown cardigan with a zip up the front, his face unshaven and unwashed, and his hair long and disheveled. Problems arose at the times when he decided to take an interest. You see, I don't know how we got here, but I remember lying on my bed with my skirts pulled up because we were playing one of those games. I think we were playing doctors and nurses, which involved a very close and very intimate physical examination of the place between my legs.

This was a secret sort of game, and it wasn't the kind of thing that you just went and told people about. No, it was the sort of game that should be kept quiet. But then what comes next is also all murky and unreal, and I am always either unable or unwilling to follow that train of thought through to its inevitable conclusion. There is a roadblock in my mind that I cannot overcome. It leaves me feeling frustrated and full of self-doubt and insecurity. There is all this self-loathing and guilt. I did something bad. I know that. It was bad. Maybe my mind has imagined this image? I hope it isn't real. God, my skin is crawling.

Like all good girls, I knew how to keep a secret, and it was one of the very first lessons that my mother had taught me. The problem is, though, that I think I might be able to keep a secret even from myself.

Charlie's ear infection didn't last forever, and one afternoon, when he was safely back at work, my mother had been installed safely back into the small, idyllic little shop. Well, I thought it was time to try and tell her something. I had been working tirelessly on my own small infantile novel, which I felt articulated all the things that I was unable to express because I just didn't have words for them. It was a book, a story with illustrations which would infer to my mother the feelings of anxiety and shame, the great fear that existed in my chest, my stomach, and my throat, the thing that I wasn't supposed to share, but desperately needed to share with some trusted adult if such a thing existed in the world. I guess I can't keep secrets after all.

Now, it wasn't always easy to get my mother's attention, but she was having a good day, so I think she felt a bit indulgent towards me, and so knelt in the thick, large cream flokati rug with her back to the real and atmospheric coal fire that was her pride and joy and looked through the small tome with I had presented her with.

'Very nice,' she said, all quiet like, which was not my mother's way.

I don't think she got that. To me, this was not some childlike scrawl; rather, it was a bound and publishable volume. She assigned no urgency to the contents, but then it's not always easy to translate the contents of your head to paper, and what I saw through her childlike perception was probably something very different to her, who thought that it was a story about ghosts. I feel like I should put something in here about reader response theory, but I think you get the drift. She talked about keeping me away from late-night television for a while after that and putting my creation in the dustbin. It was my very first rejection letter.

Sometimes in the dark and the night when the curtains were closed against the street lamps outside, and I lay listening to the swish of the cars moving on the tarmac beyond the window, well, sometimes then I could see a sort of apparition appear in my bedroom doorway, silhouetted against the dim yellow light of the forty-watt landing bulb. I would start to tremble a little in my pine bunkbed, which had been carefully selected and chosen by my mother because it matched the carefully selected and chosen bedroom furniture, separated into two twin beds, and cost an arm and a leg.

I would lie there quivering and drag the peach-coloured patterned quilt right up to my neck and wriggle backward, far away from the doorway, but it didn't matter how small or quiet or how still I made myself seem. The figure would move forward anyway and drift towards and under, and I would lay there and not breathe, and a large clammy hand would cover my face and my mouth, and I would feel fingers reaching upwards on my small short legs, and I would try to catch gasps of air between the fright and the confusion. This was our little secret.

Families always have secrets, and something changed in the dynamics of our family when we made that move to Dinnington. It was something quite imperceptible, something that would never have been noticed from the outside, something that was barely noticeable from the inside. You see, all of my short life, the family, the social group, the unit to which we had belonged, well, this had included the grandmothers. We were just one big happy family, and everyone else, everyone else including anyone belonging to the paternal family, they were the outsiders and were not to be trusted. Those were the ones for which we reserve our overly preened kind of public image, that carefully honed reputation meant that for the world outside.

Now, I relied on intuition and close observance to pick up on the particular codes of conduct that my mother would decide on, and what confused me the most back then was that when Charlie came, and we moved in with him, well, all the rules seemed to change. You see, my mother created another social group for us, a nuclear family if you like, a tight knit sort of close little unit that was made up just of us three. I knew that he was not my real father because my grandmother told me so, and I was reminded periodically by visits to my paternal grandparents and comments from my mother about my actual biological heritage. Never mind all that, though, because new and unspoken structures had been delineated. My mother, Charlie and I were the family. Now, everyone beyond that was an outsider.

My mother taught me how to keep secrets and she

taught me that family comes above everything. But she also taught me that family is not a static concept. Oh, I put my family above everything, that is for sure, but not the one that she would have me prioritise.

XIV

EQUO NE CREDITE

(Do not trust the horse)

Happiness is one of those abstract concepts that have been pondered by the great thinkers of our time and past time for time immemorial because happiness is not an easy sort of concept to define. We may experience happiness in different ways, and yet some say that happiness may be measured, it may be gauged, it may be described, it may be quantified, or it may be categorised, and it may, more generally speaking, be related to other abstract concepts like the feelings of satisfaction, contentment, and pleasure. Happiness remains strikingly conspicuous, or so we are led to believe, being marked by a certain willingness to help others, a cheery sort of disposition if you like, characterised by the upturning of one's mouth into the open and infectious gesture of a smile, a skip in one's step, and a light-hearted sort of air. When a person is happy, well, then they may maintain a disproportionate kind of enthusiasm for even the most unappealing activities but a certain degree of positivity for that to which they are able to demonstrate some ability or at least a predilection. We are easily able to recognise happiness in others, too, not through the realms of psychological surveying or subjective indexing no, but just through a quick and easy glance.

I think that I am happy, that this is what happiness is for me. A quiet sort of freedom from the nagging and persistent torment of insatiable apprehension and discomfiture, from incessant fright and intimidation, liberation from the tether of their all oppressive regulation. If happiness can be different things for different people, then for me it may be defined by an absence of something rather than the presence of something else. In their absence, I am content.

Alone with my thoughts, I have pondered the idea of happiness. Alone with no one around to intrude with their wants and needs and demands on my cogitation and that ever-dwindling amount of energy, that spark of life. I would sit for a while in my own mind and be with the words and the images, and the neurons all buzzing around in their complex little patterns and pathways as I focussed on the matter of happiness and other related material, of course, because it seemed like an important thing to consider. The matter of being happy, or at least not being unhappy. Why, I wondered, did their happiness depend on my unhappiness? Why so this interdependency? Why?

But then I'm told that this is where we come to. We often come to the question of why, in those contemplations, those deliberations, the troubled introspections that make up our time alone. And by 'we,' I mean all of 'us' who find themselves in a similar situation. This is not my story; after all, I am only one of many.

One in four women living here in Britain are subjected to sexual abuse at some point in their lives. They told me that, too. The woman you talked to in the supermarket yesterday, the one with the kind smile. The little girl you teach at school. How about that teenager acting out at the bus station? Do you wonder how she got the bruises?

We're all wondering the same thing. We want to

know why. Why me? Why them? Why her? Why us?

Because he could.

Now, as always, we start with the mother, my mother, a girl entirely dissatisfied with her own mother because Cathy held a firm and lifelong sort of belief that Joan had always put her own needs before those of her children. I couldn't say for sure not being around at the time, but I do know that my grandmother worked hard managing small businesses when many women were bound to the house, managing laundry instead, and I was proud of her for this. She always maintained that she needed to uphold her family financially because those first years had been something of a struggle for the young couple, setting up on one wage in the small northern town where they lived and with little in terms of support from their respective parents. She was putting food on the table, is what Joan argued, but this was just another source of tension and disagreement between her and my mother, in what was a very long list of contentions.

I think Cathy was just the kind of person who would never be pleased with whatever kind of life she led, largely because she never felt much in terms of contentment and always coveted what others had. I have never glanced my mother's way and thought her truly happy, not one time. But then Cathy would argue that life had dealt her some low blows. Either way, she often felt that some injury or wrong had been brought towards her, and just one of the offences that she listed in relation to her mother was that she had not been encouraged into after-school activities. I'm not joking around here; she bore this as an example of inadequate parenting for all the days that I knew her. My mother did love a pity party.

You see, she felt, Cathy, that is, she felt that she would have naturally excelled in any venture undertaken and that her life would have been considerably different if only she had been awarded the same opportunity as others clearly had, or at least those that she chose to compare herself with. Well, having a daughter of her own meant an opening to set that particular wrong right, given that she saw me as something of an extension of her own persona. An annex, if you like, a small appendix or addendum to the more dominant central character.

So, she decided to involve me in an activity that she

harboured a particular interest in, which, of course, was the norm of our relationship, where I would be expected to live out the fantasy for my mother to live vicariously through. This was how she came to sign me up for ballet classes without word or warning. She loved the grace and beauty of the dancers and knew instinctively that if she had been given such chances early on, then she would surely have been a professional by now, leading a very different existence. All I knew about ballet was that I had some pretty big shoes to fill, and it caused me some anxiety when I considered just how I could possibly be as good as my mother could have been if only she had been a spoilt child like me.

I had expressed no curiosity towards dancing, and the lessons were long and arduous. Being small and young, I struggled to keep up with the older children and didn't display much natural ability that I can honestly remember. But all these things aside, I tried my very best to please the watchful Cathy, who had dressed me head to toe in pink taffeta and would be there at the sidelines, unlike many of the other parents, offering encouragement in the form of demonstrative instruction and constant reprimands. The ballet was certainly no leisure activity.

Naturally, my mother ensured that I was put forward for the associated exams, regardless of recommendations from my teacher. We practiced and practiced. My mother and I practiced until my legs were sore and my arms ached from being held outwards in some awkward curve where my elbows could be no higher than my shoulders. I passed the exams with flying colours, but the tiny amateur board gave feedback that I was not smiling enough during the procedures, which set my mother off in a torrent of abuse and rage for days. She even bypassed her rule about public conduct and started right there in the changing room so that everyone could see me receive a good, long, and severe scolding because she'd found that humiliation was particularly effective in certain circumstances. I was six years old at this time and prone to emotional outbursts, so of course immediately began sobbing big, embarrassed tears with my face all bright red and stinging with the shame of it. There were all sorts of promises made about future performance that I honestly could not keep. I was sorry, though, genuinely, because

I'd been so focused on getting the moves right that I'd forgotten to pretend that I was enjoying myself.

My mother didn't take me to dancing classes much after this so I never did get the chance to make it up to her, but I can honestly tell you that people still comment on how lovely my smile is to this day. That was another valuable lesson well learned.

In truth, the series of admonishments that accompanied these dance lessons never helped me to improve any, and even as an adult, I feel so painfully self-conscious in any similar circumstance that I will avoid such conditions entirely. So, all in all, it was money down the drain, as Lizzie-Anne used to say. But some good did come from all that falsification of gratification, so to speak, because I became very, very adept at simulating the outward appearance of happiness to the extent that I can almost, almost convince myself. Yes, I can light up the room with a smile and still be crying on the inside. My life is a fucking sham.

Anyway, there is a point to this interlude, and you may be wondering just what that point could be, but the point that we have been waiting for so patiently is to say that I think it possible that I may have appeared happy at least some of the time and certainly in public when I was growing up.

Indeed, people would comment on how over-indulged I was, and my mother would throw elaborate birthday parties and pile up the presents all wrapped in bright shiny paper and big colourful bows. This being of course, a sure sign of her devotion to the maternal role, and not at all because she liked to put on a show, oh no. And, of course, my mother would run around frantically complaining incessantly about the duties of motherhood, and everyone around would sympathise and praise, and she would soak up the attention and snap impatiently at me whenever I walked within five metres of her about how fucking ungrateful I was. Yes, it was all about me.

And my bedroom would be filled with all the new toys and bright things after I had painstakingly removed every piece of paper at a super slow speed and played with each gift for several minutes so that I did not appear ungrateful in any way. My mother would do this, pile the items carefully in one corner as a kind of display for viewing. Anyone who came to visit would be given a tour to see the great stack of gifts so that they may also see how spoilt I was and how ungrateful I was, but most of all, how wonderful my mother was. Eventually, after several weeks of this spectacle, I would then be allowed access to the gifts at intermittent times, meaning that, unfortunately, not all items would ever be used since I would eventually just grow out of them. That was okay, though, because that way, they could be sold on and would fetch an even better price if they remained boxed.

Such was my idyllic childhood that I even had the stereotypical pet rabbit, a lonesome creature who existed far from the house in a sort of hideaway area that also contained my swing- set. It was much later than this story, later than blue flashing lights and the shrilling of the telephone, and the stopping of the shrilling, and the nice friendly counsellor. So much later, when me and my Mum, old now and all wrung out, and trying to piece together bits of her life for the support worker who came from the Crisis Intervention Team after another bad night had happened and the neighbours had finally had enough of her abuse and filth. Well it was then that she remembered some weird particle from the long forgotten, like a flake of peeling paint had fallen away to reveal something only she could see, some part of the wider puzzle. They had forgotten to feed the rabbit. 'They' because by then she mainly spoke in the third person about any aspect of her past.

'What!' Horrified. I was absolutely horrified. When I reached in my hand and, it was all stiff and cold, and the soft grey fur had lost its warmth and friendliness. They told me that the neighbours didn't like us and had poisoned the rabbit. That was what they said.

'Well,' she said, 'it was just a little white lie.'

I'd accepted that so easily, intentional sabotage by jealous neighbours, because I knew by this point that no one on the outside could be trusted. It was exactly the kind of thing that I would expect of 'them.' When I learned the truth that day, it cut me to the bone.

Don't trust strangers. Smile pretty now. Never talk about home. Don't answer questions. Remember what happens to kids in care. Don't make me look like a bad mother.

Why?

Because she could.

Despite having such a well-coached kid, it would probably have been unrealistic to expect a young child to behave quite so unnaturally for long periods of time. But because our maternal family had moved away, and our only contact took the form of pre-planned events that involved carefully illustrated precursory tutoring sessions, sometimes covering a span of many days and intensifying in activity leading up to the visitation, well, the stance was easily maintained.

It was different with Charlie's family, but they tended to remain at odds with my mother or my mother at odds with them, and either way, it only surfaced on rare occasions back in this phase of life, given that they also lived some distance from our relatively remote location. The couple had few friends between them, certainly none that would frequent our family home other than those that were associated through employment by Charles, and I can't say what they made of us seemed to matter. Still, there did remain one thorn in the side.

My mother had retained some communication with my paternal family. In fact, she was in receipt of a small maintenance allowance, which had been more recently established in the form of a standing order payment by Adam, who was now in a more stable place in his life and showing prospects for the future. Indeed, when we made the move to Dinnington, she did so with the full knowledge that my grandparents, Adam's parents, lived in a small village very close by. My mother was no quitter and didn't give up people easily. She held onto Adam's surname all of her life, even after a remarriage. I have never known what to make of that.

Anyway, being as she was, it was natural that she would use me as leverage. So, occasionally, she would spring a surprise visit on her past in-laws with the pretence of taking me for a visit. I would get shoved in first towards the door, all scared and small, and told to get on with the knocking.

'She wanted to see you.' I didn't even know who they were.

On one such occasion, I was placed firmly on the real oak kitchen table right in front of the older woman's eyes:

'Do you know who I am?' she asked in a kind but overly pronounced sort of fashion.

I was unaccustomed to being approached by adults and afraid to answer questions for myself, but my mother was giving me a look from behind this lady's back, so I did my best to get things right.

'You're Mrs Pendle,' I answered. And Mrs Pendle laughed delightedly back at me, which was fortunate indeed because my mother looked like she might be about to blow a gasket.

'No dear,' exclaimed Mrs Pendle, 'I'm your grandmother!' Well, this was news to me because I had never considered the prospect of there being more grandmothers out there other than the ones that I already knew about. At least the reason for these visits made more sense now.

Anyway, it didn't last for long because sometime after this, Cathy and Charlie took me out in his old blue van for another surprise. The day was a particularly bad one, with torrential rain battering down hard on the old metal roof as we sped along through country lanes toward some unknown destination. It was a dark sky, all foreboding and grey, with clashes of thunder streaking on the horizon. When Charlie stopped in a farmer's track metres away from an old stone building that sat within a rolling landscape of corn crops and paddocks, I was more confused than ever and more than a little apprehensive.

'Go on, guess,' my mother was crooning. I was clueless and it didn't go down well.

'You stupid girl.' The usual form of attack began, so I started brimming with rising floods of panic and a squeezing sort of tension in my frontal lobes, being all trapped like I was in the van with them.

As was inevitable, I did not manage to guess, but despite the irritability and general feeling of discord at me having ruined their fun, they continued on with the event anyway. They liked to play games, but I was never very good at them.

This was how I became introduced to pony trekking and another after-school activity that filled up my weekends, but the small, local riding school was suspiciously close in proximity to Adam's family home. It presented the perfect opportunity for my mother who would interrogate me after every lesson.

'Did you see their house?' 'Was there a car outside?'

'What kind of car was outside?' I didn't care. For one thing, it usually amounted to very little in terms of information because I wasn't even too sure which house belonged to them and would just respond in ways that seemed satisfactory. Most of all, because I became so enamoured with the idea of horses, I noticed very little of my environment and focused almost entirely on the experience. It was a frustrating time for my mother.

One day, after such an event, she asked Charles to drive us to see Mr and Mrs Pendle so that she could show me off in my riding clothes and remind me which house was theirs. Well, you know what they say, 'Do not trust the horse.' Anyway, we arrived unexpectedly, as usual, and Mrs Pendle explained that they had a small family gathering and that Adam was there with his new girlfriend, so she thought it best that we did not come in. My mother stood humiliated and furious as the white-painted wood closed quietly on her red stiffening face. I didn't really understand what was happening and hadn't developed an emotional connection, so I couldn't understand all the fuss as she dragged me back up the driveway by my arm. When we got home, my mother was raging and shocked at this unforeseen injury, so I was sent straight upstairs and out of the way so that she could make phone calls to Joan in peace and weep as she relayed the event, with Charlie down there trying hard to placate her.

It was a few years later before I was even told what had occurred, and when the news was finally imparted, it was done so in order to illustrate the harsh rejection that my mother had suffered at the hands of my paternal family.

That day, my mother decided that the Pendles would have no further access to me. Rumours were circulated by Joan to a scandalised audience that pronounced Cathy as the victim of this new and brutal outrage.

'Poor Cathy,' the horrified gossip would whisper, both inside her head and outside of it. Oh, she had been hurt that day. She had been cut to the core to see her husband move on so quickly. It was an unexpected insult, and she had lashed out in retaliation because she had control of something that she thought they all wanted. Well, it was quite a shock when they didn't contest because, of course, they had bought into the idea of me living some idyllic sort of pony trekking, ballet dancing, spoilt kind of over-indulged, loved too much life within our little family, and they thought it was 'for the best' to leave well alone, being as things were with my mother.

So, there would never be anyone checking in from that side of the family, and I would just have to muddle through. Later, Joan would say defensively that at least my mother had stuck around as if this granted her some concession for all that bad behaviour. It could have been worse, in Joan's opinion, although I tend to think that it could have been better.

Now, please don't get me wrong because I do feel grateful for my life, and growing up, I felt grateful for each small smile and act of kindness. But it was always difficult to know how long the approving sort of mood would last and how long it would be before the deep and hollow melancholy would wash over my mother again or when the explosive fury would be unleashed. Then the house would become dim and dark and fearful, and afterwards, there would be a sort of absence of spirit about her, as she sat staring into space as the sun went through its cycles and she remained unmoved. It was difficult to predict these fluctuations and even more difficult to live with them.

Still, though, that is not to say that Cathy was entirely neglectful in her maternal duties, of course not. When I was struggling day after day with discomfort and pain that made me flinch and squirm whenever I tried to urinate, well, eventually, I went to my mother about the problem.

It was never easy to get time with my mother alone, to capture her attention for long, but I remember making a sort of strategic manoeuvre to catch the woman when it was just the two of us and then managed to draw her into the small guest room with the little white vanity unit, and the carefully chosen Laura Ashley wallpaper with the small pink roses that she was so very proud of, all of which existed right at the end of the dark long landing hallway.

I explained, ashamed and contrite, trying to substitute the words that I didn't have with gestures and such. My mother stopped the conversation before it went any further then applied antiseptic healing cream to the parts that were bruised and sore.

From that night, and for some time after, I slept in that special little guest room at the end of the hallway, even though all of my things remained in the room with the hand-painted rainbows and the toys piled up, all bright and abundant.

Cathy told people that the noise from the street disrupted my sleep, and I agreed because this was true. This would often be the case, that there would be some nugget of truth to my mother's claims. It made her more believable.

XV

OMNIA CUM PRETIO

(Everything with a price)

Cathy always held some contention towards Joan, but despite that, the older woman remained her greatest advocate, a most tireless supporter of Cathy's goals. Between them, they had a way of bending the world to their own liking through the most painstaking and diligent sort of home-grown publicity campaigns that Vyacheslav Molotov himself would have been proud to claim as his own. I think that my grandmother had an instinctive sort of need to control, and she acquired dominance of her smallish clique through the dissemination of earnestly crafted and unscrupulously drafted knowledge, lore, and, quite generally speaking, information.

It was validation because what does the world consist of, if not an animated mesh of interactive and dynamic social connections with associated intelligence? Why everything else, the inanimate, is really just fixtures and fittings.

Joan knew how to spin out new realities. She was the creator of worlds, my grandmother, she weaved ontologies like some grannies knit Christmas jumpers. She would speak to a selected crowd with certainty and conviction and then leave these lesser personalities to substantiate her allegations for the purpose of authenticity. You know how people like to talk. And as much as Joan was Cathy's chief endorser, so was Cathy a primary corroborator to Joan.

Yes, Cathy was something of a champion to my grandmother, and this earned her the approval that she so desperately craved. Cynical as she was towards the woman, she would always back Joan up. It was a strangely symbiotic sort of partnership.

Late in life, when all that was going to happen had happened, and Joan's circle had become small and tight, netted slowly over time and selected for the ease of their assailability, she would draw them near and hiss at how Cathy and Charles had been soul mates: one heart living as two. Even Cathy believed her mother on this matter because, by this point, nothing much stuck from her own mind except those jumbled-up pieces that didn't quite come together. She relied almost entirely on Joan's memory to fulfil her own, and my grandmother had a way of speaking with such authority that the things she said became so.

'He was my soul mate.' My mother would repeat, 'Oh, he was a wonderful man.' Her face was all dreamy and doe-eyed. But what benefit this particular noodle might be to Joan was always a puzzle to me. I suppose we cannot know what drives another's mind.

I observed the relationship between my mother and Charles, close up, so to speak, while Joan was eighty or so miles away. Not that my memory is infallible, but from the depths of recall, the arguments and tensions that come back to me would call into question my grandmother's proclamation.

I also remember my grandmother's early reticence towards him. What I don't remember is a kind word spoken.

Back in Dinnington, after the fateful day with the

fateful discovery and the fateful move to the room down the hall with the Laura Ashley wallpaper with the small pink roses, well, it seemed that Cathy, my mother, had just put the matter to the back of her mind, having neatly resolved the situation. My mother was always very adept at misplacing things in the dark cavern of her psyche, and pivotal information could become missing in the jumble back there like it was a spare set of car keys. It might not see the light of day for decades.

I think that she might have struggled with this one, though, and it reared its ugly head in all manner of vexation and her usual frustrations with my younger self. Once again, here I was, causing her problems and destroying a most advantageous arrangement. The voices that came and went these days, well, they appeared to be back with some vengeance on this particular subject and were all abuzz with their accusations and recriminations. If you are wondering how I might know, it was in the way that she would sit for a time, staring into nothing with a strange sort of look about her face, accepting no input whatsoever.

In the end, it was a collective agreement that forced

her hand, and after seeking some advice from Joan, well, she approached Charles. Carefully, of course, tiptoeing around the subject, not wanting to cause offence. We mustn't upset the suitor.

Now, it was around this time that I can recall the numerous squabbles and arguments between the couple that, in hindsight, seemed somewhat unusual, seeing as they had become recently engaged with some large and flamboyant ring all crusted in fat blue shining jewels.

One night, soon after Charles had surprised my mother with the ring that she complained was not the proper sort for such an occasion, well, things became so heated that he actually put his fist right through the glazed French door that led from the living room to the small garden patio area. I was stuffed away upstairs again, but I knew about it because I had come rushing down at the sound of broken glass, remembering it from our previous home.

Well, it stopped my mother from shouting, that was for sure, and Charles, whose face had been all twisted up the way he got when they were wrangling, or he was angry over some perceived misdemeanour, his expression changed quickly too. He went all white, and the blood was all red against his skin. He didn't like seeing blood, I think, or something like that.

It was late and dark outside, but we all clambered quickly into his old blue Ford Transit van as the gore seeped into an old dirty tea-towel that my mother had wrapped around his wrist. He drove us to the hospital, but my mother had to take the wheel a few times, and the van swerved between the lanes as we sped along, which made the event even more frightening because we all lurched about in the front.

'Don't faint, don't faint,' my mother kept repeating. He was all over the place.

In the hospital, I got tired, and all I remember is something about stitches and something about keeping quiet because they were saying he slammed the door to close it and missed the frame. No one asked me anyway, and I fell asleep in a chair.

My mother would barely look at me anyway after the whole changing rooms debacle, then when she was called into school over some picture or something, that was it. She never said a word. And for my mother to be quiet, well, that was an unusual thing indeed.

Anyway, it was sometime soon after that another big change came about that was all sudden and quick, with little time to prepare. I was informed quite bluntly that we were leaving again. My mother told me in her hushed tones like she was imparting some arcane intellect, that Charles' family didn't like us; they thought that she was a 'slag' and a 'gold digger.' These were new words to me, but I got the gist.

They were relentless in their accusations, and she just couldn't take it anymore. It was his father, in particular, who didn't approve of the relationship, and their constant berating was getting Cathy down. If it were not for me, of course, then everything would have been perfect between them, but as it was, they considered my mother a woman of loose moral fibre and a possible threat to their family fortunes. They could not trust a woman who had a child from a previous relationship.

I felt ashamed and confused about all this, and knowing it was all my fault made me feel guilty for something that I didn't really understand. They were always so nice. Charlie's mother had big yellow hair and a lovely smile. She talked to me and gave me things to eat. I guessed people could be like this: nice to your face and nasty behind your back. I came to expect it even.

It had been some time now that I'd known myself to be substandard, inadequate, defective, inherently bad. I just wasn't sure why. At least I had some answers. It was because I didn't have a father. I was unwanted. I was an unwanted child, and at least my mother stuck around.

Anyway, in regard to this big change, she told me and others the same story. Charlie owed her twenty thousand pounds, and he took the money from his business.

It was 'her money' and 'what she was owed.' I have been unable to understand why she was owed this sum or, where it came from, or why he had it and could give it away. The matter of the money is an outright mystery, so at this point, I would invite you to speculate because that is all I have.

It was about 1985, and so my mother took this fortune and secured property at auction in the small coastal town where the grandmothers lived. God alone knows when because I certainly can't remember her visiting the place or suddenly getting a feel for the property market. But the next thing I knew, we were moving. And we moved quickly. We moved quickly in the dark. We grabbed and stashed stuff in the back of that old blue van, leaving most of our belongings behind. Most of our clothes, our furniture, the bright toys, and also, of course, our lives. All gone.

If anyone ever questioned the strangeness of this, then I wasn't around to hear it, and of course, Joan, my grandmother, would be ready with an explanation that set the world to rights. She was good like that.

Now, my mother was the kind of woman who liked to get her money's worth. So, she bought the house cheaply and in a state of desperate disrepair. It was a large five-bedroom Victorian terrace over three floors, which she believed could be worth considerably more after extensive refurbishment. I guess she also believed that she could perform such refurbishments.

There was almost no plaster left sticking to the walls so that the ancient slats beneath protruded outwards, and a chill would rustle around the place even on the warmest of days. The floors were bare wood, but the kind where tacks and large, ragged wood juts out in the corners so that shoes had to be worn at all times. It must surely have remained empty for a long period, given that the smell of mould and dank was pervasive in every way, clinging to the nostrils the clothes, and sometimes it seemed to the mind as well.

There was no bathroom to speak of, although we were able to use the toilet. We would use the bathroom at Joan's house or sometimes Lizzie-Anne's, and often, we would spend our evenings with these old matriarchs because it was nice to be around the warmth and comfort of their fire.

Since we had no beds or furniture to speak of on our arrival, having left most of our belongings behind, we spent weeks camping in one room downstairs, selected because it contained some archaic gas fire and was the only place that we would get warm. My mother strung up an old flowered sheet across the room, and we hunkered down on our individual sides in the dust and the gloom, constantly in fear of the giant arachnids that haunted the place.

It was nice to see the grandmothers, though, and truthfully, I think that I was becoming accustomed to a degree of instability. I don't remember really thinking much of it, not even when the full-sized snooker table arrived courtesy of Charles and in lieu of any other form of furniture. I was not a child who was easily surprised. And not being easily surprised was probably a very good thing because my mother didn't last long in Hornsea, at least not as long as she'd obviously planned.

Joan always said that she needed a constant kind of companionship from my mother. It was her way of explaining to me some of the more questionable decisions that had been made over the years, either by my mother or on her behalf. Well, I suppose that Joan was probably right, being privy to some additional and exclusive knowledge about Cathy that she was never prepared to share. Anyway, this need for companionship manifested itself at first in a disproportionate sort of dejection that filled the large property with a downcast gloom. It was like the shadows of some disconsolate spirit were filling the old place up, and I would jump through my skin sometimes if I saw some dark contour out of the corner of my eye. It gave the place an altogether eerie sort of feel.

Initially buoyant with grand ideas and plans, Cathy never lifted a finger in terms of redevelopment and always had a handy excuse for anyone who might question this dereliction of duty. Money, time, me. Mainly me. They would roll off her tongue like coins in a penny arcade because she had learned her trade well. Joan, feeling protective of the despondent form that passed for her errant daughter, would, of course, repeat the justifications to make them so. It was the only support she could offer. The situation was a complex one. It wasn't so much that Cathy didn't still retain these aspirations; it was just that when left to her own devices, she would lack any form of determination or focus. She needed constant encouragement to maintain momentum.

You see, Charlie had not moved with us. He would visit sometimes on the weekend. And sometimes, he would not. My mother explained this through the unpleasantness of his family towards her, and my grandmother repeated the stories, and so the tales became so. But oh, did my mother miss him or miss having someone around? She could not abide her own company, or mine for that matter.

Something else she could not abide was work, and I'm not sure how it came about, but she accepted employment working in my grandfather's little cafe. He had bought a small business near the front, which was part of the whole retirement plan. I'm not too sure that she wanted the job, though, because she was so sullen and disinclined towards the work that it was almost all she spoke about. It was petty complaints and constant remonstrations, morning, noon, and night. In fact, nothing about the place was to her liking, except the weekends when Charles would come and flash his new cars and a fat wallet, bringing sought-after prizes for my grandmother, who was furnishing a new home and appreciated not having to pay for it, Charlie, of course, being in the furniture business.

Whatever had happened back in Dinnington, Charles, with his big smile and easy ways, soon won my mother over again, and that whole mess was put behind them. Cathy began to feel like she had made a mistake with Charlie. I couldn't tell you how she felt towards me because I barely set eyes on her, except before school or after it.

It was those voices, you see, that would hiss and hurl their accusations and abuse. Oh, she would sit there with that smile on her face. I would be watching television or playing with a doll. My mother would just stare, vacant and dispossessed, far, far away, as the voices chatted amongst themselves. Until Charlie was due to arrive, of course, and then suddenly she would get up, excited, full of energy and alive with anticipation, and she would look towards me in some strange way because the voices had told her what she needed to hear.

Maybe in this way, she managed to convince herself that I was just a girl who told lies. Because I knew that very suddenly, I was more at fault than usual, and her attitude towards me changed abruptly. I was spoilt, possessive, jealous, and didn't want her to find happiness. Not to mention being a girl who made things up. It pleased her to have reached this conclusion, and I remember her relaying the information to Joan at every available opportunity as I played on the floor beside them. Joan, of course, relayed it to others, and it became so because that is how the world worked.

'Poor Cathy,' they all whispered, 'After finding happiness.'

My grandmother would be delighted when Charlie arrived with some new furnishings for her bungalows. No cash ever exchanged hands, but still, everything with a price.

Anyway, we had only been there a few months when my mother and grandmother began to circulate another story. This time, Charles needed investment for his business, and so the property in Hornsea would be sold. My mother was always selfless like that.

With that, the house was sold again, and the money poured back to wherever it had come from under the condition that my mother would see a return for 'her' sacrifice. As far as I can remember, Joan approved heartily, given that it would secure a future of carpets, beds, and mahogany trimmings for years to come.

Lizzie-Anne was older now and somewhat despairing of the situation; she thought little of Cathy's alliance and even less of Joan, but she offered to take me at weekends, and so the deal was made.

This was how, before we had barely begun life in

Hornsea, Cathy had whisked us away again, this time to a new location entirely, because a different house was purchased much to Cathy's liking, now in the centre of Rotherham. Detached, close to a park, with a large green garden. Yes, Cathy felt like she had finally arrived; this was where she was meant to be, and she adapted her personality according to these new circumstances, selecting the appropriate apparel.

Of course, dreams made of nothing more substantial than words and wishes crumble easily, and so this, too, was destined for failure. But for a time at least, Cathy had what Cathy wanted, and life was good for Cathy.

XVI

SI VIS PACEM, PARA BELLUM

(If you want peace, prepare for war!)

Not all of us have the kind of healthy, well-adjusted relatives that adhere to expected behavioural norms through concessional agreements. Some people that we hold dear will appear to wilfully deviate from social etiquette to a degree in which their demeanour becomes harmful to those around; they are outright anti-social. And this antagonism can lead to our own distinct distancing as we make the painful decision to remove ourselves from the inevitable conflict that surrounds their dysfunction.

Family estrangements are far more prevalent than is commonly thought or acknowledged, but living with such disaffection can result in decades of emotional paralysis because the society around us does not easily condone ostracism as a resolution for such grievous discontent. Indeed, maintaining connections to one's biological kindred, even in the most exceptional of circumstances, appears wholly supported and often encouraged by the values, customs, traditions, and the very core on which our wider community is based. This leaves us, the dispossessed that is, with an inalienable, uncongenial, most vehemently unpalatable sense of guilt and shame that can never be unshaken. Because family comes above all.

But what is 'family' anyway? Surely some social construct, some manufactured thing, some idea of biological unity and how that unity should look? Why does the family exist at all?

Genetic predisposition? Like some innate tendency, some biological partiality towards the proximity of shared deoxyribonucleic acid? Surely, it's not all in our DNA.

Is it instead a collective sort of assumption, a disproportionate belief if you like, an infinitely repetitive practice that has its roots in the ancient tribal history of humanity? It must be some inherited convention that we should maintain connections to these small groups into adulthood. Custom or tradition leads us to cohabitate based on biological or marital contracts and obligations, enforcing lifelong bonds for the purpose of procreation and then preserving these alliances in the interests of nurturing the next generation until maturity and beyond. We are the slaves of convention. Herodotus tells us so.

Perhaps it stems from an innate need for protection since children are dependent on their carers for survival and remain with their parents until a jointly agreed age made appropriate by the confines of the wider community, whereby they move out, but not on, retaining, maintaining, and sustaining that pre-established connection in the form of social gatherings and pre-arranged festivities. Like one big, long John Lewis Christmas advert, the family just keeps on going from one generation to the next. 'Honour thy mother and thy father,' ah, but 'they fuck you up, your mum and dad.' The cycle perpetuates and, above all, is perpetuated. Because family increases GDP, Mother's Day, Father's Day, Birthdays, and Christmas all present excellent retail opportunities. Estrangement is no friend to profit margins.

Not all of us, though, could rely upon our progenitors for that all-important early years nurturing. And we have a choice to make. Either perpetuate a different cycle: spend a lifetime in the unfulfilled angst of unrequited love directed towards the parent or parents of our hearts, desperate for some signal of approval that will satisfy an unconscious hunger for the perceived preservation that we so urgently require as infants. Or move the fuck on.

So, it is the case that there are those of us who rebel against custom, against the odious nature of our nearest and dearest. We subvert expectations. We undermine the dominant narrative and challenge the establishment. We endure the punishing sanction of expulsion, banishment, and all the associated disgrace of exile. Our failure is limitless. The mnemonics are boundless. We do not collaborate or cooperate in state-endorsed calendarized festivities, and we are not permitted the indulgence of forgetting. Because the ideal family is both aspirational and standardised, and we reckless abandoners not only lose our kinsmen but also all hope of ever achieving the fantasy of belonging, of being wanted.

From Easter to Christmas and far beyond, there remains the ever-flowing torrent of bedazzled, beaming airbrushed bitmaps radiating back at us from every magazine stand, TV screen, and neon billboard advertising both the virtue and the commonality of the modern family in all their extended glory: family meals, family parties, family gatherings, family picnics, family homes, family hobbies, family values, and revered above all family time.

It does not matter what they did; what they did becomes irrelevant.

Worry about what you did because you walked away. Worry for your own salvation. Forgive, and ye shall be forgiven.

Forgive, and they will like your selfies on Facebook.

Back in the here and now, I did not forgive. And I am not forgiven. It is my yoke to carry. 'What are you doing for Christmas?'

'Just a quiet one.'

'Does your Mum live close?' 'No, it's just the two of us.'

'Have you got any kids?' Forgive us our sins, for we

also forgive those who sin against us.

Five long years of remaining quite conspicuously, quite deliberately, quite assuredly estranged from my mother and my grandmother, who themselves, I hasten to add, remained quite estranged from me also, but of course, this part of the equation is often overlooked because it was I who did the walking. Whereas all they did was the hissing and the spitting and the lying and the biting and the backstabbing to anyone who would listen. But their abuse is nothing, nothing when compared to how I walked away. If you want peace, prepare for war.

Living in exile wasn't something that I ever really talked about much. What was there to say anyway? I was always so conflicted on the matter. On the one hand, I appreciated the stillness and the calm: it was a freedom of sorts, a liberty, a kind of buoyancy if you like, without those constant and somewhat overbearing insinuations. Like the fault finding, the pervasive negativity, not just about me, but other people, too. Those dark and indistinguishable moments that left me drained and soulless. It was bad to listen and worse to join in. Afterwards, I felt the old, creeping, shameful feeling crawling along my arms and, down my tightening throat and up toward my face. That would be hot and red, and my head would pound with regret and remorse.

I despised myself for having been so needy, so desperate for some moment of validation. Disapproval, manipulation, coercion, judgment, disparagements, denigration, outright slams. Sometimes, I participated, sometimes I was targeted. All times, they were the result of any direct contact or, indeed, indirect confrontation with those that I optimistically described in Hallmark terms as my loved ones.

Lead us not into temptation.

On the other hand, when it ended, I felt the great and overwhelming loss that comes with closing the door to people who represented such a large emotional part of my life. I was hopeless and bereft, like a bottomless well of grey melancholy resided deep inside, and every day brought with it just another attempt not to disturb it, an exhausting trial of survival with no possibility of reconciliation or resolution in sight.

Living is a heavy burden when you carry around the weight of having hurt someone you love to some immeasurable degree, not knowing if they will ever recover. There could be no closure, no end to the depth of sorrow that I carried with me, and, furthermore, no opportunity to heal. The grief was overwhelming.

'Happy?' My bear-like husband would ask, seeking reassurance over some project, some DIY or cooking thing.

'Hhhmm.' I would mutter back because what else could I do? This was beyond his measure of understanding and had dragged on for literally years. It was shameful the way that I could lie my way through the day, concealing any real emotion, unwilling or un-wanting to share this part of myself. Jealously guarding this pit of dark sorrow against potential intruders.

It would be fair to say that Cathy and Joan also felt conflicted by the conditions of this separation, albeit though on somewhat different terms. These two women lived their mature years in the awkward position of feeling threatened by and jealous of almost all familial and social connections while at the same time requiring a sort of exaggerated sense of substantiation and attentiveness from the very same people that they would openly admonish. Of course, this often led to hostility as the person of their current interest would become confused, drained, and shockingly distressed by the indomitable force to which united this unlikely pair seemed to make. So, over time, it was inevitable that the hyperbolic sense of entitlement that was generated and maintained between them would just sort of rinse those around of any kind of energy, life force if you like, or indeed will to abscond, almost as if some dark creature of the night had ensnared and secured that person as their unwilling victim. But yes, the long years of rejection and alienation did indeed take their toll, as somehow, they had to find a way to manage the feelings of shame and inadequacy that arose as a result of this unforeseen rebuff, and then, of course, supplement the loss of this perceived affection with some other. Family estrangements are a difficult time for everyone.

Cathy and Joan never were the kind of people to pass up on an opportunity, though. For them, the internal fractions of our family dynamics also represented a time of careful and industrious planning. They had begun their campaign of misinformation and defamation almost immediately, a preoccupation that was born from fear, as the shocking realisation that such an asset was now no longer within their control began slowly, at first, to sink in. It was with some urgency that they assigned the task of ensuring that their falsifications remained the only version of reality that the small network in which they resided would ever accept. Because, after all, the truth was neither here nor there for these two. They spoke in forked tongues, these women, and made honest and open relationships impossible. They didn't want a daughter or a granddaughter, no, what they needed was a collaborator, and I had resigned from the post. It's not like the relationship had ever really been an easy one, but after that night, that oh-so-awful night, well, those misrepresentations that I had somehow managed to live by all came tumbling down, and I just could no longer ignore or deny them. The truth was screaming to be heard, and the truth cannot be denied.

Perhaps then, it is with some degree of wonder that you might accept the next part of this story, but I will try and tell it as it happened. Because you see, despite all of this, in spite of all of this, knowing full well how things would be and how things had been, in full knowledge of what I would encounter, I actually went back. I made the metaphorical journey from my world to theirs. I ventured back to the place of subtext, imitation, and callous insinuation. I attempted a reconciliation. I must have been out of my mind.

Nevertheless, this is how I found myself. Dazzled by the light, and wondering how long it would take before the minions were dispersed. The flying monkeys. The prologue, if you like. Because Joan was nothing if not a Master of Composition.

'Someone should write a book about my life.' She used to exclaim during a particularly heartfelt soliloquy in which she would recount her many perceived misfortunes.

Well, I hope this is to your liking, Grand-Mama. The day of my return went something like this: First, they came out pleading.

'Give it time, give it time.'

There were tears, you see, in the house. There were always tears. She was hurt, she was wronged. She'd told her side, false accusations, recriminations. But she spun a compelling yarn that year on year wound more complex and elaborate so that its intricate patterns rested gently on the world like a soft veil, shielding those dark, ugly truths with lurid imagination. And shrouded beneath the soft tendrils of its roots, I remained choked and silent. Quiet, complicit, desperate. Desperate to tear open the frail fabric of lies but afraid of Joan's hidden wrath. Best to find a free place and make that my own. Let the sun fall on my pale skin and breathe the soft, clean air. But now I journeyed back beneath the webs, and already it was stifling.

So here they were explaining as if I needed telling. I could have told them if they'd had ears to listen. But they were under the spell, and reason had no place here. Joan was crying. That was enough to force an interjection. Those tears were like an elixir that coerced others to do their bidding. And accordingly, her minions came to meet me, those vassals, those flying monkeys, if you like. Perhaps she would see me, and perhaps she wouldn't. But I knew, and she knew, that the opportunity could not be missed.

Everything was in place. The stage was set. The audience watched her every move, and they could not be disappointed. She must play her role flawlessly. They fluttered and fussed. She sobbed and hissed. And outside her latest confidant, the one she called a friend, recounted the words that she'd been entrusted with, should such an occasion arise.

'You haven't seen the worst of it. Not by any measure. But she's been there through thick and thin. She's hurt right now; she has a royal fury. But the waters will calm. Best you don't enter. She said she won't see you.' The words they fell empty around us, scattered like dried leaves.

They were nothing to me. I already knew the plot, I'd seen this drama unfold before and read the play a thousand times. My part was irrelevant because Joan always held the limelight. I could stay and try to reason or leave right now, but the performance would continue as planned either way. The lines were pre-written; they were as old as time itself. So, I entered the lion's den, knowing full well what to expect.

Joan was holding court, the performance in full

swing. It had been years, but the words came with unexpected ease. I consoled, I cajoled. Those dark eyes were milky now with age, like mood stones; they shone polished and pearlescent, quickly changeable, stormy as the weather, heavy with their secrets.

She told her tales well to a spellbound audience, and most left convinced. She had lost none of the charm and none of the malice. Her old gold looked brassy, but she didn't seem to notice. It clung to her cinnamon skin like armour as she flung poisoned words with the skill of a seasoned assassin. Old gold and flaking eyeliner. This is all that was left. Old gold, eyeliner, and the precision of her aim.

Quiet reasoning provokes confrontation, though. I know that well enough. Fear is a powerful force. Doors slammed shut to steady the tide of flooding reality that my soft words brought.

Act Three and I tried to deflect the blows with love, but the bruising began to smart. Joan was afraid. Backing into a corner like a wild thing. Less guarded now.

When I had left years before, I'd dragged baggage behind, a suitcase full of secrets. My gems. Little ears and little eyes listen and see well. She'd imparted her treasures to me, and now here I was, my pockets stuffed with hand grenades.

Reputation was everything. Now was the time for damage control. So, we reconciled with conditions in place. Because Joan would have her power returned, one way or another. Slowly, the world slid back into her predetermined order. She spoke the words and made it so. Threads moved gently into place. Others repeated her mandate, and the pattern began to emerge. Contradictions only spoiled the careful tapestry, but with care and dedication, she would unravel those tangled threads and weave out a new story. She had the time, and she had the will. Her ingenuity must be respected.

This was how I was granted access to my mother, who was being carefully protected now, carefully controlled.

She was happy in her bedlam, Cathy, smaller somehow, a tiny creature of squarish dimensions, who moved around quickly and purposefully, peering still through those round brown eyes. Seemingly unsteady, she tottered here and there with furtive glances to all around, some imagined, some not. Truth be told, she was glad of the additional company, although those voices helped to fill the void left by the ones that had fled her hot temper and oscillating unpredictability. Having something more substantial to converse about over trivial matters and small talk gave her a radiance of disposition that my grandmother hadn't seen for some time. It pleased them both because Joan really did have her daughter's interests somewhere in that dark, bitter heart.

However, regardless of my input, the duo maintained that odd, symbiotic sort of attachment that led to such consternation and utter frustration for those involved. Cathy would walk every day to Joan's home, taking her small dog, her constant companion, her raison d'être. Joan would complain at the pair, fuss around, and generally rankle, giving her also some purpose in that small and lonely life. When not together, they talked on the telephone, sometimes several times in the hour, and otherwise criticised one another heartfully and fervently to any who would listen while privately clinging to their bond for the very particular kind of support that only the other could offer. It was a mutually disadvantageous sort of relationship.

As for me, well, I had lived for years by this point in the shining light of truth and veracity, and to submit once again, to yield myself to the diminished, to the corruptible, to the delusional world of my mother's making, and grandmother's sustaining, well, it was an impossibility. With every clash, every mismatch, every incompatibility or skirmish, I would feel like a part of myself had been lost, like I was fragmenting, like a component self was tearing and shedding away. I was nothing more than tissue paper on the breeze, slowly withering into obscurity.

Notwithstanding, though these most personal reverberations, I had returned for one very singular, very calculated kind of purpose, and I had absolutely no intentions, despite the implication to my own mental or physical health, from being dissuaded. So, regardless of the hostility and rage presented by my indignant grandmother towards this one distinctive goal, I continued resolutely in pursuit.

Now this motivation of mine was probably more

rooted in self-interest than altruism, but this only became clear to me later in some momentary illumination. My one purpose was to ensure that my mother received the kind of medical care that it was so very evident that she needed. Back then, I really thought that we could be a family again, a kind of cakes and coffee, shopping trips at the weekend, chicken on a Sunday sort of family. The three of us, though, not just me and her. Grandmother, daughter, granddaughter. The way things should have been if only Joan had left us well alone or done the right thing long ago.

This was the idea that I clung to on those dark, long nights of self-doubt and deprecation, and I was more than prepared to fight my own dear grand-mama for the dream of it, even with all her spurious allegations and spiteful manipulations because I believed that I too was the kind of person who could make things happen. I am ever the fool.

It is a most undesirable chore to fill out the blanks of your chaotic, tumultuous life, Mother, which is my own chaotic, tumultuous life, too. We continue unabated in that same pre-determined trajectory, gathering momentum and additional force, like a cannonball rolling down a steep and nefarious incline, occasionally coming into contact with some innocent bystander or other. Collateral damage. When I think of what could have been, then I lament for you, Mother, I mourn for us all.

XVII

ABBATI, MEDICO, PATRONO QUE INTIMA PANDE

(Conceal not the truth from your physician or lawyer!)

In my own unqualified and highly biased opinion of the matter, there appears to remain a somewhat fervent and enthusiastic distaste in those less forward-thinking types towards mental health complications that no amount of publicity or subliminal prime-time TV messages can seem to eradicate. It's like admitting to suffering from mental health problems is somehow comparable with something disgraceful, a debauchery of some kind. I've experienced this myself, like when I told my grandmother how the doctor had prescribed me anti-depressants, and she said:

'Well, just snap out of it, girl, just you snap yourself right out of it!'

Like I had some choice in the matter, I always was a disgrace to the family, but they made it clear this time that

I had gone too far. We need to do more to help people, that is for sure. Because just wringing out the obligatory social script of condolences, those old familiar lines deemed socially acceptable but that so often mask more unfavourable thoughts on the subject, which are then voiced in the comfort and privacy of people's homes and family, well, I just don't feel like it's good enough.

Despite what might be said to the contrary in the national newspapers, for instance, there remains a stigma associated with mental health illnesses that is deep-rooted and not easy to dislodge. Such matters can be seen as an outright slur against the family. Why, my grandmother would not hear of her daughter receiving help in this area, she would not entertain the notion that it was needed. So, in her refusal, denial, and closeted shame, she set a course of events in motion that would cause significant damage to others.

It is a crying shame to my mind when such a foolish thing as a little self-consciousness becomes the root cause of a person not receiving urgent medical care, but Joan was always the type of person who would put her own needs above others. She spent her life obsessed with what others might think of her. And this was always really the story of Cathy's life, this undercurrent of paranoia and self-consciousness that was driven and actively encouraged by Joan. Poor Cathy, indeed.

But then I spent five years in exile, and five years is long enough to change a person's perspective, and it certainly was long enough to change mine. When I saw my mother again, it came as quite a shock.

All those little foibles, those idiosyncrasies if you like, those eccentricities that I had been encouraged to laugh off and not question, well, I realised very suddenly on that very first visit, with not an underwhelming level of disturbance, that these habits amounted to something more. I felt stupefied. I just felt outright stupid. I don't know how I could have lived all those years and not realised something like this, something as plain and obvious as the nose on my face. It was much the manner in which my mother spoke more than anything, which was no different at all from the way in which she had spoken to me for as long as I can remember, and much unlike my mother, I can remember quite a lot.

One time, for instance, long before this, when we were all sitting around my grandmother's dining table, and she was putting on some spread, some Sunday lunch or Easter Monday kind of dinner for us all, and we were laughing. Yes, we laughed. There was love and laughter, which might sound strange given the circumstances, but ours is a complicated sort of story. She was there then, of course, I mean my light, my life. Young and fair, she had big grey eyes that danced and sparkled as we all laughed together because that is what she loved best of all. And her hair would fall over her shoulders and shimmer like spun gold in the afternoon sun filtering in through the large French doors. She was such a lovely thing to be around. Maybe this is the reason that we all laughed and loved back then. Maybe in the bright illumination of her grace, we were each something better than we are because when she left, she took the laughter and the love away with her, and the room seemed dull afterward, dim and musty even on the hottest July day.

Well, my mother came out with one of her classics because they were arguing about the internet again, her and Poppy.

'She says it's the devil!' Poppy exclaimed, rolling her exasperated eyes towards my mother accusingly. We all laughed heartily, and my mother looked about her sheepishly, like she'd been caught out.

'I watched a documentary.' She was getting all indignant now like she did, defensive. We laughed again and let her keep digging.

'They said that W.W.W is equal to 6.6.6 in Hebrew,' she explained, 'and that is the sign of the devil, so the internet is the devil,' as we all rolled around, she glared her small brown eyes towards my husband who she tended to associate with computers and the internet in general because of his job. My grandmother tutted on from the kitchen.

'Oh Cathy,' she admonished, then 'She's just too tight to pay for it,' and we rolled around again, laughing some more as my grandfather told jokes about moths and purses.

'Mummmm,' she called, 'They're picking on me, tell them,' and my grandmother came in to half-heartedly threaten us, thus becoming the new target of our heckling, which shut my mother up but, of course, her mood had changed to sullen by now, so it was too late.

'The sun'll come out tomorrow. Bet ya bottom dollar that tomorrow there'll be sun!

When I'm stuck with a day that's grey and lonely.

I just stick out my chin, grin, and say, Oh!' She warbled in a young child's voice with a strong American accent. This time, my Grandfather intervened, turning to my husband and asking about the last formula one race while me and Poppy helped my grandmother in the kitchen. Because we all knew any interruption would turn my mother's mood hostile, and the day would be lost. Best not to confront it. Best to ignore it. But I never questioned what 'it' was.

In the end, I did what I always did and took out a contract for a broadband dongle so that Poppy could have internet access at home, bypassing my mother altogether.

Once she had an idea in her head, there would be no getting around it. Honestly, I thought no more about it.

When I went back, she was living in what appeared to be a nice, cosy three-bedroom semi-detached red brick-built property in the bustling seaside town of Bridlington, nestled on the East Coast, close to where her parents had eventually retired, after finding the smaller more rural settlement too tight-knit to contain Joan's spurious comments and megalomaniacal sense of grandeur. Although they were in near proximity to one another, Joan remained vehemently in denial of her daughter's condition and never under any circumstances, entered her tiny dominion, the small home that she had made for herself. This way, when she was told of its current disorder by me or anyone else, she was able to conclusively declare us liars, retaining instead the picture of how it had once been more than eight years ago when she had last entered the premises.

The gardens and paths to Cathy's little kingdom remained unkempt and overrun, and there were thick, dusty, well-worn, well-faded curtains hanging closed from each window against the brightest of days. All in all, the property had a feeling of being deserted, and yet there inside, she remained with her small dog, peering from between the hangings, watching the comings and goings, talking to the others, the others that only she could hear and see, and living amidst the confusion of her untreated, uncared for raging psychosis.

After a recent incident in which a kindly neighbour had opened the door to find Cathy wielding a hockey stick aggressively towards her, there was some reason for this mistrustful and overly suspicious woman to feel a certain amount of persecution since, despite Joan's soft soaping of said neighbour to prevent the assault from being reported, news had travelled fast, and people were indeed whispering all around. Still, the unexpected surprise of a daughter that she had no memory of had been enough to lift my mother's waning spirits, and she began to prepare for my regular visits with some anticipation. And I would also prepare, but instead, with feelings of apprehension and overwhelming trepidation.

In the morning beforehand, I would sit in the car and force my body to react in a manner that would begin the somewhat challenging kinetic process of moving mechanisms and dials, wheels and pedals so that I could drive the vehicle and begin the eighty or so mile journey to where my mother lived. Halfway there, I would undoubtedly have broken down into tears, shaking at the wheel, unable to feel my hands, wrists, and arms, as the steady and by now familiar feeling of rising depersonalisation began to envelop me, along with the creeping sense of fear and failure.

I was afraid. Afraid that I would lose myself there and then to the tingling, throbbing, immense, sweeping feeling of my mind trying desperately to depart towards some position of safety, some shelter in this emotional tidal storm that represented any meeting with my mother and grandmother. My psyche seemed to be clamouring for an escape from the inevitable danger of the encounter to come, and I tried with all my might, all my resolution, every fibre of doggedness that I possessed, to fight it. All sense of purpose at this point honed into the one singular action of not retreating backwards, which was really the only sensible way forward. No, I was going to see it through and do the right thing. Well, by the time I made it there then I would be absolutely exhausted. And that was just the start of my day.

Then I would tap on my mother's fully painted glass front door, which was not actually intended to be the entryway to a person's home, but of course, Cathy had not been dissuaded from the possibility when discovering the item at a cut price, having bought this property too in need of entire renovation. Well, now, she regretted the matter, being someone concerned about the possibility of intruders and prying eyes, so she shielded herself with another large, obtrusive, and dusty thick curtain, which she would squint from, usually ten minutes or so after the knocking had commenced because she had no memory of my numerous phone calls reminding her that the visit was today.

On finally bypassing the numerous security features, some of which involved bungee cords carefully and elaborately woven from the front door handle to the banister rail, which would surely only help an intruder to gain access, well then I would be supplied with a cup of strong tea, which would be undrinkable given that the house smelled entirely of stale dog urine, and the cup along with it.

I would usually have stepped in some fresh urine or possibly something worse on my way through to the dimly lit canine-covered lounge. And all through the house, everywhere and on every surface were the memorabilia of my childhood, glaring defiantly through the grime.

After attempting some form of tidying, cleansing, polishing, disinfecting, or emptying of the fridge and it's out of date mouldy contents because Cathy had absolutely no sense of smell, no sense of the year, no sense for being able to manage her home or her health, well then we would receive our instructions for the day from Joan, who saw the visits as an opportunity for a number of chores to be accomplished so that she might enjoy some time to herself, still feeling somewhat burdened with the responsibilities of a familial role.

She would, of course, deign to endure my company for an hour or two if the mood would take her that way but complained incessantly about it afterward while making comments that would naturally cast aspersions towards my credibility and ceaseless remarks about the great love affair that was Cathy and Charlie. What a wonderful and gregarious man that Charlie had been, and what a terrible crime to humanity his early demise represented, and what a monstrous child I was to my mother and Charlie, and how my most abominable behaviour had most likely caused Charlie's early demise, and my mother's ill health now.

Yes, I have much to answer for. But usually, I would just sit in silence and let the lies buzz around my head like fruit flies flapping at the glass in summer. Although, unlike the flies, I had less hope of ever getting through.

Now, it was quite clear to most outside of this self-revered inner circle that Cathy required attention with urgency and speed, but Joan would hear nothing of it. She considered this daughter, this first-born, to be something of an insurance policy, representing the help and aid that she would need in those twilight years. Apparently, a deal had been struck long ago in some late-night bargain. So, with this hawk like presence controlling all the cards and Cathy's natural fear of those in a position of authority driven by Joan's unscrupulous manipulation of her vulnerabilities, well acquiring medical expertise on the matter was no easy task to accomplish. In the end, it is fair to say that I received much help in reaching this goal, and I am very grateful to all those involved.

When I was eventually able to present Cathy to a local physician, he had not seen the woman in more than a decade and her medical history was somewhat dubious from before then anyway. Conceal not the truth from your physician or your lawyer, or so they say. But of course, Cathy learned from Joan that she should conceal the truth from almost everyone.

Well, this physician, having read the notes and seeing some interest from another practitioner, declared on the spot, so to speak, that Cathy had no capacity to make decisions on her own account. The proclamation came when she outright refused treatment for her mental health once again and with the same strong vehemence to which she had been making these rebuttals for many years. You see, Cathy refused wholeheartedly to accept there being anything wrong and instead projected the condition onto others.

Sometimes we would be walking down the street, and she would hiss at me: 'Look at that nutter!' with her face all twisted in disgust.

Usually, it was someone going innocently about their business, fortunately, oblivious to these accusations, and I was never really able to discern what my mother perceived in them.

But anyway, as you can imagine, she was all colours of livid as this authoritarian figure signed the paperwork and made instructions there and then for a third party to become involved and get her the kind of treatment that would categorise her once and for all. He asked me my opinion, and I was in agreement, giving evidence, so to speak, of some of her more irrational speculations and delusional behaviour. Well, the look on her face is one that I will never forget. I had betrayed her, and I knew it. After all these years of keeping the family secrets, I'd finally made some admission. And here I go, making a few more.

She picked up her bag and left, and afterwards, I found her outside on a nearby bench.

'Am I a nutter?' was what she asked me, small and muted.

I was trying not to cry. 'You're not a nutter, Mother,' I didn't lie because I don't believe in that word. 'You're a person who needs some tablets and talking therapy, and you'll be right as rain, just like me.' I didn't lie because I totally believed it.

'And then we'll be a family again, me, you and Poppy.' Jesus, how could I have been so fucking naïve?

My grandmother found out about the betrayal, too, and you can imagine the outrage. After all, this was her physician also, so already there was at least one person outside of the family who knew. She made an appointment immediately and asked him to stop the process, and as far as I understand went week in and week out with the same request and allegations towards me and my intentions. I'd like to say she drove herself insane with it, but I think that boat had sailed long ago.

Anyway, a few days later, a small white vehicle turned up outside my mother's home with clear blue NHS lettering that made it quite visible to all as to what the nice talking nurses were there for. And my grandmother became hysterical. She was on the phone sometimes three or four times a day to me, threatening me, threatening her own life, threatening all manner of things, pleading with me, pleading for my mother. She was not about to let this disgrace be known, but as it happens, there was nothing that she could do, or I could do, once the ball got rolling. This was what angered her more than anything I think, because she had lost control.

She was relentless, and after a while, it began to feel like some kind of war was taking place, like a continued battering assault. It felt like she was trying to destroy me, and I was never in a position to defend myself because I loved her so much. It was a metaphorical assassination, but in no way less deadly, and truth be told, to me, it felt quite literal like some slow-working malevolent poison had entered my system and was steadily running its way through. Some venomous acrimony to which I had no internal defences. An assault of slanderous misrepresentation and murderous libel, the besmirching of character by the toxic tablets of lies mixed in a liquid of seasoned reason that Joan spat like sparks across her social network until they turned quickly into wildfire that spread untamed between us.

Before I knew what had happened, we were entirely divided. I knelt at one side, crying in the scorched earth, burnt and frayed, unable to tolerate the heat of this continued abuse and, above all, the abhorrence she had towards me. It was utterly absurd, the things she came out with.

My grandmother won in the end, I guess. However, I don't know what kind of victory you would call it. She had won a battle of her own making that she had conducted like a military strike. She tried every trick in her handbook, calling me such names like liar, degenerate, thief. In the end, I listened, and that was the day that my husband found me collapsed and unconscious on the bathroom floor. It was a point of no return.

So, I went away again because what other choice was there? Cathy lost her daughter again and for good, and Joan, her granddaughter. You can't have one without the other. Me, well, I realised that you could not lose what you never had. So, in some ways, their loss was my gain.

I will never forget the last time that I saw my grandmother, though, oh how I loved her. She was framed in the canopy of an Edwardian seaside home, green ivy trailing around the brickwork, and the sunlight filtering gently in the sycamore-lined street. As the seagulls called out to one another, she stood waving in the doorway, and I was waving back. She had a strange look on her face like she was trying to hold back the tears as she watched me drive away, and she had set her mouth into a firm but insincere smile. I knew at that moment she had guessed that I was saying goodbye for good because her face reflected mine perfectly. It's the hardest thing in the world to deprive yourself of someone that you love, but sometimes you have to sacrifice your heart so that the rest of you can go on living.

XVIII

MATER ARTIUM NECESSITAS

(Necessity is the mother of invention)

Rigid and smiling is always how I sit. I was taught to sit this way from being the smallest of girls. All stiff and polite with a neat floral bag on my knee. And this was how I discussed the inconvenient matter of incessant and explosive rage boiling up inside of me, like a poster child for Miss Manners.

My therapist, god bless her, she tried to help, suggesting various techniques at first, like scribbling angrily with a pen and some paper.

"Just let all that anger out," was her advice, "throw things around the room, scream into a pillow. Do what works for you." But none of these things did work for me because of all that freakish self-discipline that my mother had beaten into me way back then. I could not do it. I could not vent.

When I was a small child, my aunt used to complain constantly at Christmas and birthdays about how slowly and carefully I would peel the wrapping paper from my gifts. How studiously I would examine each present before moving to the next. How delicately I would remove each piece of sticky tape. It would drive her wild.

"Just open the damn presents," she'd be calling. But of course, my mother would have taken me aside afterwards and shown me just how ungrateful a child I was, had I not demonstrated due respect and restraint.

Restraint like this is not given up easily, and still, today, I cannot scrawl wildly on a piece of paper any more than I can rip a parcel open with intent or raise my voice in anger.

A smarter person would turn to drink in my situation, but truthfully, I think that I've become afraid of letting go after all these years of composure. So, maybe I didn't really want to be helped at all. Nevertheless, I'd sit there and pay close attention anyway. Diligently complete my diaries. Think through the day and hold onto any small fragment of contentment. Talk about his fucking, dirty filthy flesh of on my thigh and the taste of bile in my mouth. What I didn't really talk about, though, was being totally desensitised, numb, and deadened, like my body was just the physical shell from which I could view and access the world around me. Honestly, sometimes it's like I exist elsewhere. And only in this state, this state of not really being present, am I ever able to manage the memories that manifest themselves from nowhere and bubble up to the surface, refusing in their stubborn way to sink back down again.

'And how does that make you feel?' She would ask.

'I think I feel ashamed.' Sometimes, I would make up the associated emotion because I was too anxious to be sure of anything and the shame place is always a safe bet since I spend so much time in mine that it has taken on the appearance of an Ikea show home. Throw cushions, scented candles, fluffy rugs. Cosy.

Sometimes, she would look at me in an odd way, and I would panic and retreat further into the subjective distance of my intellectual confinement. A place that I had created in my own mind long, long ago to provide an interval of remoteness between myself and anything too overwhelming or threatening. Back away, back away.

I'd always hoped that in releasing the inner dialogue, I would find a way to escape this self-imposed internment. She asked me what kind of person I was, and I told her an optimist.

'Just call me Pollyanna.'

Even sealed in the sanctuary of psychotherapy, I would still search for some reason in the madness, logic and intent. Even here, I was their greatest defender, balancing the good with the bad, determined to faithfully, if not fairly, represent their characters. I clung to any small beneficence. Gave credit where credit was due. Convinced myself that I was loved.

Maybe that was why I would find myself winding and weaving back to that house by the park. It was a pursuit for some glimmer of affection.

This was a time most favourable, most prosperous for the small and afflicted family that we were because it was here that my mother was the happiest in all the time that I remember. And although we didn't live there awfully long, I always look back on this brief period as something of a golden time, a time of what could have been.

Part of the reason for the fondness that I have towards these recollections was that whether by chance or by circumstance, my mother's behaviour became quite noticeably different from the outset of our habitation. And she was different towards me in many ways. For one thing, I was offered the great privilege of accompanying the couple to their viewing of the property, which also afforded me the opportunity to meet a girl who would later become a classmate. This was a rare sort of inclusion and preparation that was not usually attainable but resulted in my knowing both the house and at least one individual at the dreaded new school when the move was made. It is still appreciated.

During this viewing, Cathy and Charles were in full swing, giving their absolute best performance of a happy and family-oriented partnership while I was left to adventure through the garden with the current owner's children. I got the impression that my mother quite liked the idea of small ones playing on the lawn while she fluffed about somewhere indoors because when we left the place that day, this was what she had become. Some sort of 'Respectable-middle-class- housewife-working-part-time-for-pin-money-and-sanity' type, whereas in the morning, she'd still been 'Dejected-poor-Cathy-divorced-single-mother-living-on-benefits.'

I always saw it as some kind of survival skill that my mother could change with the wind this way. Necessity is the mother of invention and all that. Whereas People like you and me might select an outfit for some special occasion, my mother can apply a whole new character which just happens to have an accompanying wardrobe.

Her costumes could be convincing, though, so much so, in fact, that I think Cathy herself would believe wholeheartedly in their authenticity, making their portrayal all the easier. I like to imagine that she takes inspiration from popular culture and media characters, embeds within them something of herself, and then makes the suit adaptable to meet the needs of the ensuing situation. Even the last time I saw my mother, she could still assume a few of these roles with ease and flare, hiding her own vulnerabilities behind the guise of this new or old appropriation.

Back at the house next to the park, though, I think she felt intimidated by the lady of the house and required a distinct shift in outlook from the downtrodden, downcast and downhearted Cathy that tends to be her old faithful. So, she became the buoyant and successful homemaker who would mark this new phase of her life. Simples.

I remember it as being just the fresh start that my mother needed because this new persona came with a sort of infectious vitality. She was also a bit on the indulgent side too and much more maternal than the last. So, the alternation did not perturb me in the slightest. Being around nine at the time and perfectly accustomed to such modifications in my primary caregiver, this was my normal. Besides, the change represented a new beginning for us all.

When we did make the physical transition, well, I found the house to be large and comfortable, having such things as plaster, wallpaper, fixings, and even carpets, which made it a veritable palace compared to the derelict property in Hornsea that we left behind us. In truth, I was happy to leave the old, unrenovated shell and its giant eight-legged occupants in the past, although I soon felt homesick for those fussing grandmothers and the small school with the friends that I had just started to make. But much like the transformations of my mother, I was also growing accustomed to instability in my surroundings: friends, schools, teachers, classrooms, hobbies, the walls that we lived in and the beds that we slept on. I didn't give starting over a second thought because I had come to understand life as being transient and unpredictable, and I accepted this without question.

Now, because my mother is one of those people who has a shortfall where her self-esteem should be, our new home was much more about her own validation than it was somewhere to live. She was insecure, underconfident, anxious, and mostly preoccupied with raising her perceived appearance in the eyes of others. I think she visualised how they might see her, sort of projected an image of herself that existed only in her own mind's eye and then imagined that this was the image that they would see. It was the image that my mother focussed on with intensity. Her life was about improving this image, the reputation of this image, the value of this image, an image that only she herself could see. She did battle with this image day in and day out, and battle with anything or anyone that might threaten it, like me.

Of course, those around us were absorbed with their own lives and didn't have that much interest in ours, but my mother would never have seen it this way. The new house, with its landscaped gardens and large driveway, was a boost to her fragile pride and ego because she tended to derive her own value and worth, or maybe that of the image, from what she possessed, having been taught this by Joan at an early age. So, she now felt ten feet tall. I swear that she visibly grew in stature during the time that we lived in that house and shrunk immediately again when we left.

All those belongings, the furniture and toys, clothes, and trinkets that we had deserted in Dinnington late one evening, well, they all found their way to the new home and were carefully placed and polished by my mother. She decorated each room one by one, spending hours and hours deciding on colours and wallpaper, putting her stamp on the property as a homemaker might. Then the relatives were invited, and we cleaned and tidied and cooked for days beforehand, pretending, of course, that we lived like this all the time.

My mother basked in the light of their compliments, now in her Laura Ashley blouse and mohair. And I was careful to sit rigid and quiet, following the strict instructions she had given me not to leave any mark of my childish whims, no toys on the stairs or where straying eyes may see them, no evidence of my existence at all. Otherwise, there would be all hell to pay when they left.

Regular inspections were made of the room that she described as my bedroom to visitors. The one which was full of expensive soft pine furniture from one of Charlie's shops, that was all very easily marked or scratched so could not be played with or near or on. Also, it was made clear from the outset that it all belonged to my mother and was only being loaned to me so that I had somewhere to sleep and didn't need to be taken into care. It had been easier to navigate the old derelict building in Hornsea. Nothing in that house had been classified as 'Valuable.'

After the visitors left, the routine went with them and we were able to relax again. My mother could never keep up with the housework for long, so we were soon in our usual disarray, which was much more normal.

There was a smaller room that Cathy liked to call my playroom, and so long as no one was expected, I could sleep in there too, which was better for me with it being cosy and more child friendly. Also, full of things to do. My mother loved bragging to her relatives about how spoiled I was, having two bedrooms and all that. In truth, that other pine room meant nothing to me and was just somewhere she could go and sit in from time to time in order to admire the décor and dream about some other kind of child she might have been lucky enough to have instead of me. Life was never kind to poor Cathy.

She was a complicated woman and led a complicated life, the intricacies of which are often still too difficult for me to unravel. My grandmother used to tell me tall tales about her ancestors, and I think that my mother believed in them, thinking that she was owed some sort of position, some sort of birthright, so that this house and the security that went with it, gave her a kind of position or status that she felt was her due. At the same time, though, I think she also felt the fragility or brevity of any sort of achievement and was forever attempting to protect what she had worked so hard to attain from some imagined attacker.

Sometimes, it would be the spurious and often manufactured accusations of Charles's family, and at other times, it might be her own relatives. Whether the allegations were genuine or conceived, they still caused her a large degree of distress, and so to counter any claims to the contrary, she would ensure that it appeared as if we benefited very little from any income or wealth that Charles might have.

I think it was paranoia over this perceived financial status that led to her obsession with tabletop sales, second-hand shops, and any other kind of bargain hunting that you can dream of. I can't remember a thing of mine ever being bought at full price, and it was rare indeed if it was new at all. She would make out to Charlie's relations that this was down to our being destitute but lie differently to ours, bragging heartily of the spoils of Charlie's success.

This subterfuge would result in a complex set of falsifications and associated coaching before any visit. It was always easiest just to keep my mouth shut in order to avoid confronting one of my mother's fabrications head-on. Even as an adult, I have found myself staggering haphazardly into 'misrepresentations' that she had planted twenty-five years or more earlier and still not rebutted. Just a few years ago, there was an unfortunate conversation with my aunt that left me in hot water regarding another property in Rotherham.

'Well, they were struggling with the mortgage payments, weren't they?'

'But they didn't have a mortgage on that house. They paid outright.' The stony silence at the other end of the phone told me I'd fallen into yet another landmine. It turned out that my mother had been fleecing that particular relative for decades, using one sob story after another. Why she would, I'll never know. But my saying the wrong thing caused my mother all sorts of problems.

And caused all sorts of problems for me since that hot temper would find its target as soon as said relative was out of earshot, regardless of how 'Mumsy' she was feeling that particular week.

'Mumsy' she was too, in the nice new house by the park, and living so close to a large town also meant regular shopping opportunities. I think that the harsh words of those medical professionals were still in my mother's mind, or maybe old Lizzie-Anne was nagging at her down the phone lines because she made sure to buy food for me, too. She would come home with bits and bobs like mini-pizzas, beef burgers, mousses and things from the local supermarket that I could cook for myself and from then on, I took care of my own meals. In addition, she even registered me with a local medical practitioner, which was the first time in three years. I think she must have been growing into her role as I was growing into mine.

Of course, at this point, my mother was still quite young, in her late twenties with a nine- year-old child. She had a family home to take care of and a partner with a business, all of which amounted to a reasonable amount of responsibility. I feel for her. I am sympathetic to this person, and I hope that you are, too. One day in recent years, when we were sat in her moth-eaten living room, with the stink of stale dog urine high in our nostrils and the dust hanging in webs all around, she told me that she had tried hard to make us all a family in this new home, me, her and Charles. The new home by the park that is. We sat that day, me and her, drinking stewed tea from dirt-crusted mugs without milk because I had found her bottle all lumpy and green in the fridge. Waiting for the little white car with the NHS lettering to pull up outside and for the nice NHS ladies from the Crisis Intervention Team to come along inside and talk to us carefully about my mother's self-neglect and history of mental illness. So, we waited, and we talked about how she had tried hard to generate opportunities for me to spend more time with Charlie back then. She wanted me to like him. She was trying to be a good mother.

'We only wanted the best for you.' She told me. I believed her. I believed that this version of herself believed that she had been the kind of mother who wanted the best for her children and that Charlie had been the kind of stepfather who went out into the world to try and provide whatever that best was.

That must be why it came as such a blow back then when she discovered that I had returned to my old bad habits and begun soiling myself again. Here in this home that she had made for us, this haven of opportunity, this palace of family life. And what was worse, for my mother that is, what was worse is that I had taken to hiding my soiled underwear and garments in the hope that she would not discover the shameful act. Of course, she always did discover the incident, usually by the smell emanating from behind a radiator or some such secreted place. It goes through me now to think of it.

Jesus when she found them. How she would bring the house down with her rage and her repulsion. It was a good job we were detached, she used to say, and she was right about that because I would curl up and weep on the landing, crawling and snivelling like a dog as she waved them around and in my face. Her small, round features were all distorted and chewed up and hateful. She told me straight up how disgusting, low, and filthy I was. She held nothing back now, not in this place. What a creature I was, she'd tell me. Fucking inhuman.

'Do you want them to take you away?' She'd shriek.

Sometimes, I'd think that maybe I did. But if I spoke at all, it would be worse. All snot balls and choked sobs.

'Do you want them to think I'm a bad mother?'

I knew that I was a piece of shit; she didn't need to scream it at me. It wasn't that she was a bad mother; it was that I was a bad kid. I told her or tried to tell her. I didn't want it to happen, but I couldn't stop it either. I knew that I was unclean and shameful. Bad kid, bad kid.

'I'm sorry Mum. Please, Mum. Please stop, Mum. Please. You're hurting me. Please. I'm sorry.' I'd be blubbering, all contrite. Pathetic.

But she didn't need to hold back because we were detached now. She kicked again and again, supporting herself on the off-white satin finish bannister rail as I sobbed into the cream wool twist pile on the landing that had cost Charlie an arm and a leg. She was mad as hell that this had started up again, and she told me a ton of times that I had better put a stop to it. I tried, but I didn't know how.

XIV

EST QUAEDAM FIERE VOLUPTAS

(There is a certain pleasure in weeping)

We were most at ease with one another in this place, this home of ours with the grassy green gardens that grew beside the grassy green park, that had in it all of those mossy green trees that enveloped our little house like a viridescent canopy. Sometimes, I walk past that old house now, with its manicured lawns and the garden wall outside all rebuilt from when Charlie had too much that night and drove into it with his big SUV. Sometimes, still if the light is exactly right and the breeze is blowing eastwards, then I can glimpse her there, welcoming those simpering guests, smiling through those thin, pink lips of hers. Their eyes were bright with cosmetics, and her red cheeks were smudged with powder.

I can still remember how they twinkled and glittered with intensity, those eyes, the shine and lustre of her thick brown hair as she flitted and batted about the place, fluffing and perfecting, delighting in the bright, cosy warmth of her accomplishments as they silently reflected back in their overly polished mahogany and golden filigree glare. How she tittered towards the grandmother who came to marvel at her triumph, the older woman's eyes seeming to acknowledge that the student had become the master.

Sometimes, when I think of her, then I try to think of her being only there. I think of the better days because the worst days were yet to come.

We were at ease for a while here, though, at least, because I feasted in my childlike way on the grassy green park under the glassy blue sky and the small liberties that it represented while my mother revelled in something else. Being as she was, driven to assess the world around her in terms of its monetary value, she spent her life clamouring and scraping, wrangling, and scrabbling for every shred of tenure, asset, and every small and insignificant thing. Her happiness increased incrementally with each new acquisition, each penny saved and squirrelled.

MEA CULPA

So, whereby the hot summer days would find me lying with my back to the cool emerald shoots that blanketed our little park, gazing upwards towards the textured sunlight filtering down through the jadeite foliage above it, instead, they would find my mother hunkered down in one of Charlie's dank shops haggling with some customer over the price of a carpet fitting. My mother found her comforts in the stacks of mattresses and synthetic fibres, whereas I felt reassurance in knowing that the surrounding flora bore witness to the humdrum business of our prosaic lives. I felt less alone.

'Look after the pennies, and the pounds will look after themselves.' She would tell me as she gleefully totted up the day's takings, small brown eyes acutely focused on the banknotes. But of course, she was ever the fool, my mother, because wealth can come and go, fortune being inherently and most exasperatingly volatile in nature, and you would think that she would know this better than most. Yet in all her years, she never ceased snatching and grabbing and grubbing away in some vain effort to acquire more of those pennies and more of those pounds.

There was such vulgarity to the way that she scrabbled and clawed that I started to think of money as a cheapish and tawdry sort of commodity; it could buy you nothing of any lasting value or quality, as far I could tell. So, I would have none of it, never helping her grow those little stacks as she'd hoped I would. But then, my mother didn't like other people much anyway, and me included. She always preferred things that she could count and control, like coins or digitised transfers.

In the end, she was entirely impoverished, having lost everything that she had held dear and then everything that she had not held dear as well. Whether she missed the flesh and blood or the baubles and bright things more, I could not tell you, though, because I was already out of the door.

At least in this house by the grassy green park, I had the trees and the birds for company, and it occurs to me now, speaking as an adult, that my mother and I spent extraordinarily little time together, whether here or elsewhere. So, her thriftiness extended beyond things of monetary value. Of course, there was the business-as-usual sort of stuff: school and shopping, but mostly, I would stay well out of the way.

'Children should be seen and not heard,' is what my mother used to say, but I think that she was pretty flexible on the being seen part.

She was never the type to play games and such or get involved in childish things. Apart from this one time at the ramshackle house in Hornsea when Charlie was visiting. Late one stormy night, the three of us sat around an old Monopoly board in one of the cold, derelict rooms on the first floor, my mother squealing with delight as he cheated us both out of property rent. They had been unusually jovial that evening, laughing and dancing about the house, telling senseless jokes and falling about the place.

Why I was awake with them in the early hours, I just can't remember, but we used the table that my mother had bought me for my ninth birthday, since it was all we had at the time. A full-sized plastic green patio set with four chairs and a parasol which was somewhat redundant since we didn't have a garden but added a carnival atmosphere to the proceedings.

It was Charlie who had involved me in the entertainment because my mother was only ever about the basic upkeep when it came to me. School, essential shopping, visiting relatives, first aid. It was a relationship of maintenance. Therefore, increasingly, at the nice new house by the park, Charlie became a more prominent figure in my life. Whereas my mother might bat me away like an insect, Charlie always seemed more accessible and didn't mind the odd game of cards, for instance, or a chat about school. When my cycling proficiency came up, it was Charlie who showed me how to balance on a bike the night before because my mother had been entirely unaware that this would be a prerequisite skill for the course when she booked it or that I was lacking in expertise. Likewise, when I and a boy in my fourth-year class at junior school held hands in the yard, then it was Charlie who expressed some interest, putting a birthday card through the front door addressed to 'Mummy

Hammill,' presumably designed to warn me off a potential escalation of the romance.

A problem arose here, though, as it was not my birthday, and I didn't understand the joke. So, while the two adults stood sniggering above, delighted at the prank, I became increasingly frustrated and upset.

'You stupid girl.' Came the usual retort from my mother as Charlie began to take offence at the rebuttal. This was followed by a literal kick up the backside that sent me flying into the staircase and very nearly knocked out my front tooth.

'Get to bed.' And I was confined to quarters for most of the weekend after that to think about what I'd done and learn some respect for my elders.

So, while Charlie could often be more approachable than my mother, his affections were a volatile thing. Any perceived slight would result in her wading in to resolve the matter, leaving him smirking in the background like the cat that got the cream. On the other hand, my mother was either unvaryingly indifferent or hostile, and this was better in many ways because I knew where I stood. One thing she did like about me, though, was my hair.

'Little girls should look like little girls,' is what she used to say, and she was immensely proud of my long, brown plaits, which she would weave intricately for special occasions.

If it were up to me, then I would have liked a newer style like my friends at school, something a bit more grown-up. But when I asked, she told me, 'No chance,' and after a while, it led to some teasing in the playground because my mother was still plaiting ribbons into my locks when she had the time, and the other kids thought they were hilarious. I didn't see the funny side when she was dragging the bristles across my scalp and snapping at Charlie over my head, so it became another point of contention between us. She would tell me that my hair belonged to her since she was responsible for me until I was eighteen. I used to count the days.

Anyway, the matter was resolved between us in an unexpected way. On one of those days that all children dread, the kind where the clouds hang grey and ominous in the sky, and the rain comes down heavy on the land like a wet curtain of tiny glistening gems, the kind where they start to sense that autumn will soon be upon us, and with it a period of internment, well on one of these days I was left alone in the house with little to do. I had started to find mischief, I think, to bend the rules and push the boundaries, and in doing so, I discovered one of those unopened birthday gifts that were for looking at but not touching.

Now, my grandmother Joan was much like my mother in many ways, and instead of trawling around toy shops looking for something to amuse a child, she just packaged something from her hair salon, which was much more convenient. This is how I came to be the proud owner of a hot hair styling brush for my tenth birthday. And I can tell you that since that time, I have had great respect for hairdressers and hot air brushes, specifically because I got it wound up so tight in my long hair that I could not break it loose again, no matter what I tried. It was nothing like the marketing image on the box, nothing, and my soft brown wisps quickly became a big, tangled, locked-up mess that absolutely refused to let go of the brush.

Alone and panicking, all I could do was rock with my hands wrapped around my knees, horrified that my mother would find me. So, spurred on by this thought, I tugged and yanked while steamy wet tears rolled down my red-hot face, and then eventually, having absolutely no idea what to do to fix the mess, I picked up my cutting-out scissors and did just that. I chopped my own hair that day with a pair of oversized orange safety scissors, then stashed the evidence back into the box exactly where I'd found it. It was the first time that I had ever broken the rules, but it turned out not to be the last.

It seemed like I might get away with this demeanour the following week because, for several days, my mother absentmindedly dragged the brush through my lopsided fuzz in the mornings, shoving it briskly into a headband without noticing the missing strands. I would then hurry off to school, relieved to have survived another day.

Finally, on Friday that week, it all came to a head because she and Charlie decided to collect me after school in his big, shiny SUV. They liked to make a show of it in front of the other parents and teachers because there was no point in them owning an expensive vehicle like this unless other people knew about it.

Before I had made it into the car, she was on me, gasping like there had been a death in the family.

'Your hair!' The cat was out of the bag.

She had glanced my way when I was walking towards them and noticed that a large portion of my hair was missing from the left side, and naturally, she was furious. Fury was always her 'go-to' emotion.

'I can't believe you've been to school like that and made me look like a bad mother.' I could see that she was working herself up to a full meltdown, hissing at me pointedly from the front seat, head swung around at a seemingly inhuman angle. But of course, there were still other parents around, and she didn't want them to notice, so she was smiling and waving at the same time as performing the interrogation through the side of her thin, taut lips. She was a good multi-tasker, my mum.

'What is your teacher going to think of me?' I stammered something out about no one noticing.

'How long has it been like this?' She'd cut me off.

'What the fuck happened to all your beautiful hair?' I was trying to think fast, but the tears were building up.

'I want answers now, young lady!' Full choking sobs.

'Oh, let's not start with the dramatics.' This was Charlie intervening now, as my mother quickly wound the windows up so that the other parents wouldn't hear me crying.

'Right, just you wait till I get you home, my girl; I'll give you something to cry about.' And off we went, back to the nice detached house by the park where no one can hear you scream.

She was all manner of angry with my mother, seething red, and I knew that I was in for it. So, this is where my life of crime began because what I did, and I'm not proud of this, but what I did was make up a story denying culpability. And by the time we were home, I'd lied through my teeth in some vain effort to get her off my back, but in doing so, I dropped some other poor kid in it.

Afraid and alarmed, with my pulse racing. Tears rolled down my big, round, wet cheeks, and Charlie smirking in the next room.

But my mother believed my cock and bull about the kid up the road coming around and wanting to play hairdresser, so she dragged me around there to have a go at his mother as I stood behind her on the step, looking embarrassed and contrite. His mother was having none of it, though and ended up slamming the door on her screeching face. It was like a Greek funeral when we got home, and all that over a bit of hair.

Anyway, that weekend, she gave me a telephone number for a local salon and passed me one of the banknotes from her counting piles. I was becoming more accustomed to managing my own life, but this felt like a bit much. I walked a mile in the direction of the shop, found it, and convinced the surprised staff that it was okay to style my hair unsupervised and unparented.

The stylist tutted and muttered something under her breath to a colleague but was kind about it all and made me a cup of tea.

Afterward, my mother was angrier than I'd ever seen her because I returned home with a mullet similar to the one my friends at school were all getting. She was all colours of livid that I'd let them do that to me because she would have asked for something different, and I don't remember her saying more than a word in my direction for at least three or four weeks afterward unless to bark some command or complaint.

My grandmother wasn't very pleased when she found out either since she felt offended that we had bypassed her services. Neither of us really understood the point of what my mother had done, sending me to this place that none of us had ever been in before.

Anyway, my mother said that it had turned me into someone that she didn't recognise, and I could tell from the look on her face that I would pay for this mistake because those small round brown eyes were directed towards me, and that was never a good thing. I knew well enough not to attract attention from Cathy, and attention was an awfully bad thing.

When it came down to it, though, the matter of punishment was delayed because my mother had bigger fish to fry. It was around this time that Charlie's business, the one that she also worked in, that we counted on for income and security, well, just sort of dissolved before our very eyes. There must have been more to it than this, but it all seemed to happen so quickly, and the reasons given were so very mysterious. What had been lucrative just twelve months prior was now a matter for the administrators.

All of a sudden, the hair and such were really neither here nor there because Cathy's very carefully constructed corner of the world was crumbling around her, and she was about to lose everything that she had worked so hard to possess. Her home, her job, and her sense of self.

I can remember this happening quite distinctly, remember the Cathy that we had known for a while by the park gently blowing away again like the crisp dry autumn leaves around us. The Cathy that had been comprised of damask wall coverings and forty-ounce twist piles became like dust on the wind, adding to what had once been that canopy of green leaves, which now rustled crisp and dry in piles along the well-worn paths.

The seasons came, and the seasons went, and with them marked the passing of our lives, but occasionally also the more dramatic termination of some juncture, some position, some phase of living. That look she held in her eye, that wistful gaze, that unfettered sorrow that hung about in wisps and clouds meant only one thing to those of us around her: it was time to start over.

Twenty-four months, I think it was before the house stood empty again. Empty but for the sumptuously rich wool carpets and the decadent papers that clung to the walls in tendrils of rich bloom on golden vinyl. All the things my mother loved most in the world taken from her, like thieves in the night, had come and quietly slunk away with all her wishes and her dreams.

I walked the rooms and the halls that last empty day, a child lost in the activity of movers and relatives and my mother's hysteria. Unnoticed, I gazed through the windows, sauntered in the gardens, walked to the small playroom upstairs and ran a finger across the white melamine desk and the bookshelves, with the neat red trim and the black wallpaper with the sparkly flowers that had carried me gently to sleep at night.

My hair was cut short, but not yet a woman and no longer a child. I sat on the desk where I had written and read and worked and studied, and played with my sticky things and papers, and I knew in some way that I would not play again and that this part of my life was over. And I wept. I wept there in that child's playroom for the longest time, unnoticed and undisturbed.

My mother wept, too. She wept when they took away the fine mahogany table. She wept for the soft cream leather as it left through the front door. She wept disconsolately when the large SUV diesel guzzling machine was collected and the papers signed for, and Charlie came into the big empty house and wept too, wept like a child who had lost his favourite toy.

Me, I didn't weep for these things or for anything. I wept for the moment, for the whisper, because for the briefest time, I had relaxed in the winds of hope and promise, and it had felt good. And I wept for the feel of the green shoots beneath my back and the sunshine filtering through the leaves above. I wept for what might have been because we might have been happy. I wept for my childhood, for the loss and for the relief of it being over, and I wept for my future because I wondered what would come next.

Unlike my mother, I was coming to learn that life was a temporal, impermanent sort of affair, and all good things must come to an end, as do all bad things also. Life was a precarious sort of creature, and I was entirely at its mercy. But still, I wept because, ultimately, there is a certain pleasure in weeping.

Eventually, though, I wiped my face clean, like I had a thousand times before, and did what I could so as to continue unnoticed, like I had a thousand times before, and then I walked downstairs and into the presence of my mother's weeping like I had also done a thousand times before. Because for me, on this day at least, the weeping was over.

XX

EXCUSATIO NON PETITIA, ACCUSATIO MANIFESTA

(A guilty conscience needs no accuser)

There are some kinds of unhappiness that are so intense, so distinctly profound, that they leave behind a lingering stain. Like the stink of an obscure vile substance that stubbornly refuses to wash away, misery permeates the fabrics of life and then holds on with obstinate tenacity. This is how it was in our final abode, where the residence gradually became tainted by our woe and saturated by our dysphoria so that the walls, the carpets, the rooms, and the doors all reeked of gloom, and everyone who visited could smell its foul stench.

Even now, despite the decades, I still get the odd whiff from time to time in my nostrils and about my person. I can feel the despondency creeping in, clinging to my hair and skin, dragging me down, downwards, ever down. Sometimes I wonder, stomach-lurching and mind racing if I will ever shake off the desperation from that place. Certainly, only by force of mind do I now precipitate an excursion through the gaping distance of time back yonder into the bitter reminiscence of those last, strange days filled deeply with despair. To walk the slow, steady incline of the narrow brick-lined path, open the worn, rusting latch, and enter again that to which I swore an oath I would never return, only then to discover that the magnitude of years and space that I have positioned between us is inconsequential, because still there remains a sense of sinister pensiveness about the location and the memory of it.

This was a house so incurably soaked in melancholy that we could barely breathe but for the swaddling of malodorous discontent, and that melancholy seems somehow to transcend the boundaries of dimensional limitations because I see it now more clearly, putrid and rank with despair, what was once my home, my safety. So unlike that other residence by the park with its grassy lawns and spacious rooms, this house had a large wooden door that opened up directly into the parlour, meaning only that some effort was made in terms of making the room presentable for guests and so forth, while most of our messy living happened in the kitchen. I don't know if you are familiar with the late Edwardian terrace strip that has its staircase directly down the middle and a small bathroom upstairs, which was often added hurriedly in the 1970s when the government began to concern themselves with the manner in which people were living. Well, this was the kind of property that we are talking about, symbolic of the industrial revolution and post-industrial towns like Rotherham that sprang from it. The house itself was no more than a tiny place: two up, two down, with a small narrow strip of land at the back and a steep stone set of stairs at the front. In winter, the access was hazardous on sparkling cold streets made sharp with ice, and in summer, the smell of tar and warm diesel pervaded the place from the hot tarmac roads directly outside. We had become accustomed to more space, and the large reproduction furniture that my mother had been able to rescue from the culling looked awkward within the confines of those tiny rooms. She fetched what she could, though, dragging it along to this savage new land with the baggage of her tightly bound dreams and hopes. But looking back, I wonder now if she ever bothered to unpack.

Of course, to Cathy and Charlie, who didn't think beyond their own small lives, the house was only symbolic of how far they'd fallen, and so, like a lost people, they would move around wondering how circumstance could engineer such cruelty while much of our personal effects remained boxed in the dank, dark cellar below because they deemed this new residence to be only a temporary setback, at least in the beginning. This unlikely pair would soon be on their uppers again and in a position to reclaim all that was due. Or at least, this was the story they clung to late at night in those first few weeks and months as the oppressive darkness drew close outside and their voices fell to whispers lest any unwanted interloper should overhear through the adjoining brickwork.

So, the message was not to become too comfortable, and while Charlie went out to work for some other boss, Cathy would dream about where his new ventures might take them. There was one thing for sure in my mother's mind back then and that one thing was that she had backed herself a winning pony. She believed that Charles was a natural-born salesman, and everybody else said it was true, too, because no one wants to be the bearer of bad news. My grandfather, though, was a more grounded man, and I would sometimes see him shaking his head with disgust and muttering something under his breath while Joan rushed in quickly to shut him up. She didn't want a fallout with my mother and was all about keeping the peace, but I must admit that I respected my grandfather more for his clarity of vision.

In the end, there had come excuse after excuse for why Charlie failed to succeed at one of the big, professional sales interviews, and instead, he took the only opening available to him, which was at some local firm in Darnall selling small premiums over the telephone to the local clientele. His father, who it turns out had been the one managing most of Charlie's business all along, well, he knew the owner of the insurance place and had managed to pull some strings, so it was a pity position, really, and the pay was so low that we could barely cover the utilities since he made few sales and received little in terms of commission. Still, it gave my mother breathing room to weave a new narrative and finally embrace a different sort of existence.

'You win some, you lose some.' Charlie used to say in one of his more philosophical moods, and I suppose he was right because we lost the Cathy of our park side residence and quickly won as her replacement a more dejected and worn-down version of the earlier Hornsea model, aged far beyond her twenty-nine years. I guess Charlie was okay with all the comings and goings because he never seemed to bat an eye, but this 'hardened-by-life-and-loss' Cathy was much less decorous than the previous one, and soon I began to realise that we'd never known how good we'd had it back at that big house with the lawns. When Charlie was diagnosed with a degenerative neurological condition, then I think he began to realise that too.

Anyway, what with his doctors' appointments and hospital visits, Charlie ended up at home a lot more and eventually let the insurance job go altogether or was let go from it. I never remember which way my mother spun that one.

Needless to say, the health condition became convenient for my mother, who told anyone that would listen some cock and bull about how this was the reason that he had lost his business in the first place and how they were thinking of suing a doctor from way back who had misdiagnosed him. Then, of course it was the reason why he couldn't do a job now and why we were living hand to mouth and needed so many handouts. It also became a reasonable excuse for why he said all that weird stuff the way he did: something about causing damage to his brain and being less inhibited around people. In all fairness, no one had ever spent that much time with him before, so they just hadn't noticed that he was a few sandwiches short.

We lost Old Lizzie-Anne around this same time, and although I wasn't allowed to attend her funeral, I remember that her going left a hole in my heart that couldn't be mended, and I would cry myself to sleep at night thinking of us sat playing those dominoes together the way we did. My mother, too, seemed to feel the loss, and without the older woman's reassuring presence, her paranoia raged unchallenged and unabated, and she would smile that soft smile of hers as the voices tittered and buzzed away inside her frazzled mind, like a hive of insects nesting after the winter thaw. Meanwhile, I was left to survive on my wits, crammed into the tiny house with the both of them at home all day, looking for something to occupy their child-like minds.

'Tell her, tell her, Cathy, tell her.' Charlie would say to my mother if I so much as looked his way, and in response, she'd bark something at me and tell me to get lost in my room as they giggled together, pleased at this last thread of power.

Sometimes, he would need more, though.

'Hit her, hit her Cathy, go on, hit her. Just do it.' While he watched me intently with a smile on his face, like I was his next meal. My mother, all bucked up by this, well, she would come at me and be shouting with her face all twisted and scornful, half spite, half pleasure.

Sometimes, she would give me a kick or a push, then look back for approval while he nodded encouragingly.

Then there were those times when she was really worked up, sort of bouncing a bit on the balls of her feet and leaning forward, arms swinging, and her chubby round hands clenched into fists.

If I was on the floor, then she'd start kicking until she lost her slippers and hurt her toes on my arms or ribs, so I had learned to try for the bed because this tended to result in fewer blows. She tended to be a kicker and a pusher, my mum, although she could also wield a good hard slap if she were so inclined.

One time when she'd found me crying for Lizzie-Anne, then things got a bit nastier and after a bit of ear bashing about how I'd never cared for the old girl anyway and so must be lying about why I was in tears, well she launched herself at me, and all I can remember is her hands around my neck squeezing and squeezing and the look on her face above me all tight and red. Her knees were by either side of me, and she was bulky by this time so I couldn't breathe but for the weight of her, let alone the feel of her pudgy fingers around my throat.

Charlie was jeering in the doorway. He had a cane now and was waving it in the air by his waist like this was an illegal wrestling match, and he had money on us. She let go, but it was reluctant. As she left, Charlie rested his arm across her shoulders comfortingly, and she made appreciative noises like she needed a bit of support while I rolled over on the bed, sobbing and gasping for air.

For the life of me I can't even remember what had happened to precipitate this, why they'd come barging into my room in the first place. It wasn't like they would have ever respected boundaries or anything, and that room belonged to my mother, not to me.

Anyway, they left me lying there crying that afternoon, and I remember that I was to stay there for the night because something was shouted before the door slammed shut behind them, but the house was deadly silent in the evening, and I thought they might have left. Hoped they might have left, I guess. Sometimes, they liked to go shopping or off out to see Charlie's Mum. So, I snuck downstairs because I was hungry and still shaky from the afternoon's events. I just wanted a drink and to rummage in the cupboards for something they wouldn't miss.

Unfortunately, I made the mistake of walking into the parlour, our front room, and there I found my mother naked from the waist down with Charlie's head between her legs. She jumped up quickly but they both laughed heartily at the intrusion and made some suggestion that I didn't understand and can't remember. I started backing out into the kitchen, but my mother followed me.

She was wearing only a short, pink jersey top that came only to her waist, and I didn't know where to look. It was an intensely uncomfortable experience. I was not used to seeing my mother naked, and I snapped.

'Mother, you're disgusting; put some clothes on.' I yapped out something to this effect, and she turned around and slammed her right hand into my shoulder hard, so I fell against the kitchen counter.

'You're disgusting.' She snarled. 'You, you're the disgusting one. Do you think anyone will eva' love you? Go on, gerra out of ere, GUUU ON.' I was running towards the stairs as Charlie came hobbling through to get in on the action.

'What's she said?'

'Say's I'm the disgusting one!' My mother was outraged by this. 'Just hit her.'

'She's not worth it.'

After that, she got on the phone with my grandmother Joan, and I could hear her upstairs because our walls were all paper-thin, and she'd stretch the phone cable as far as was physically possible to the bottom of the stairs and then speak loudly at the bottom of them.

'Did you hear that? Your Mama says you're a very naughty girl.'

Meanwhile, Charlie was in the kitchen frying up chips in the dedicated pan that lived on our stove top because a nice bowl of crinkle cut always cheered my mother up.

I was desperate to use the toilet that night but didn't dare leave my room again.

Under this dark and forbidding sort of cloud, I attended the first year of a local comprehensive school, my hair still short and my uniform made up of randomised charity shop finds approximate to the appropriate colour.

In some ways, I saw education as a beacon of hope on the bleak horizon of contempt and irrationality that I experienced as the norm on a day-to-day basis, an opportunity to escape my mother's gaze and be amongst other people of a similar age. But of course, kids are very attuned to the stink of misery; they can smell it a mile away, and they know to avoid that reek at all costs. So, my comprehensive school education turned out to be as lonely and unrewarding as my home life. In the end, though, I didn't have to endure that first year for awfully long because, following a mysterious illness, it was thought best by all involved that I try somewhere different.

It went something like this: one day, I was walking around our tiny home in a silk nightgown and stockings that my mother had bought for me, which, as I write out now, seems like it may require some further explanation. My mother had started buying me clothes that were intended for adults rather than children at the house by the park. She liked me to wear red stiletto heel boots, leopard skin suits, short tops, and little black dresses. I had associated nightwear, and when we had been on summer holidays in our previous life, very skimpy bikinis, which, in the right light, would make it seem as if I had something more than an entirely flat chest.

Charlie loved the outfits and had me pose in them this way and that while he clicked away on his old kodak, flicking his lips every now and again with his red, serpent-like tongue. It meant nothing to me, except the part where I was doing something pleasing and would be reciprocated by some kind gesture from Charles and by the lack of some unkind gesture from my mother. The truth of the matter is that I was glad of the positive attention; I loved strutting about in front of that camera. I mean, it makes me shudder a bit now, but I thought nothing of it back then. A guilty conscience needs no accuser and the heat rises in my face just thinking of the way I would throw my arms open in front of that lens.

Anyway, the staircase in the new house was very steep, and the pink silk dressing gown too long, and I ended up sliding heavy and hard down several steps, my back thudding all the way to the bottom. My mother was downstairs and came rushing when she heard the fall and found me unable to move, winded and gasping for air at the bottom. All I remember now is the idea of the pain and the pink silk all wrapped around.

She got me to the sofa in the living room and laid me down while I choked for oxygen and cried through the tight, hurting band around me. Then she found two Ponstan tablets that my grandmother Joan had been prescribed for her back and pushed them into my mouth with water. I know that I slept on the sofa that night and don't remember much of the next few days because I think the Ponstans must have had a strange reaction and made me lightheaded and slightly drowsy.

After this incident, school became more difficult and I started to have problems writing. My right arm and shoulder were painful for much of the time, and my mother began to grow concerned. She was ever attentive, spending hours of her time with me, carefully accommodating to my every need, bringing drinks and food. Tablets. Keeping me in bed. Then, after a few weeks, we finally went to see a doctor, and she lied and said that there had been no injury when he asked. I went along with it because I knew better than to contradict her, especially in public.

I'd been on bed rest for weeks, and the doctor told her that I should exercise, but then my legs felt numb and heavy as well, and he ended up yanking me into the local hospital for a thorough investigation.

Well, my mother she was beside herself and demonstrably devoted to my well-being. All the staff on the ward could see what a wonderful mother she was. At night, she would come and fluff my grown-out hair into waves on the pillow, crying soft tears by my bedside, and when the nurses did their rounds, she would hold my hand and stroke my arm lest I feel nervous or ill at ease. I wasn't used to people touching me at all unless it was in anger or something worse, and this show of affection left me with an overwhelming feeling of being loved and wanted, as I had never been loved and wanted before. Furthermore, Charlie would remain on the outskirts, lurking, being snapped immediately away if he approached too closely or said anything that my mother considered untoward. He was nothing to us now.

After being in the hospital for several weeks I was asked to speak to a very kindly lady alone about all manner of things, like school and home. We talked at length about my unhappiness and why I hadn't discussed this with my mother and I tried to make up some excuse about how much Poor Cathy had on her plate now with Charlie and everything else going on. Well, the next thing I remember is me being back in bed and my mother storming down the ward, face set like stone. Very much the antithesis of her usual bedside manner.

The curtains were pulled around my bed and we had this discussion, me, her, and a nurse, a discussion about me leaving the hospital. Well, suddenly, I was very, very afraid.

'I don't want to go home.' Now, that was a mistake that I paid for tenfold.

It turned out that the very kindly lady had also invited my mother to chat that same afternoon.

'How does she get on with your boyfriend, Charles?'
Well, that one really set the cat amongst the pigeons, and
my mother had stormed out of that meeting with all
shades of furious and had me discharged from the hospital
immediately, raising hell at the nurse's station, refusing to
take no for an answer. She dragged me home that day,
upstairs to my room, and then balled me out for an hour
or more about what had just happened. I'd made her look
like a bad mother.

It turned out that although there was some nerve
damage in my shoulder, the problems with my legs were
psychosomatic, and so she told all of our relatives that
there was nothing wrong with me at all and that I had been
putting it on for attention. They believed it. She told them
all how I had lied in the hospital, leading to accusations
against Charlie, how he had been accused of 'interfering
with me.' They believed that, too. From that day on, she
told absolutely everyone she had ever met that the hospital
had diagnosed me with mental health problems and that I
was a compulsive liar. Everyone just believed her. Just like
that. Simples.

I've never been able to work out if it was about self-preservation or if she was just that stupid. But there we go. It really was the most perfect alibi.

The hospital sent letter after letter wanting to talk to my mother and see me for further treatment, but she ignored all of them, tore them up and put them in the bin right in front of my face. I was about twelve, so this was around nineteen eighty-nine, and I guess before the whole joined-up-care approach. If the case was ever referred, then I certainly didn't hear about it.

Meanwhile, Joan and my Aunt, who was a nurse, told me that they were also disgusted by my disgraceful behaviour and advised my mother to set down some discipline. She assured them that from now on, the easy street was over, and she certainly wasn't kidding about that because I think Cathy thought herself untouchable after this.

A few days after the hospital discharge, my mother had a job interview to work nights in a care home and was all worked up about going. Charlie was extremely supportive of these endeavours, but I was anxious that she would leave me alone with him and didn't know how to broach the subject directly. Finally, as my mother was heading out of the front door, the one which faced the entire street, I began my protest in desperation.

'Don't go, Mum, please, don't go.' I whispered hastily.

'What's this nonsense? I won't be long. They said an hour at most.'

'No mum, please, please mum, please, please, don't go! Please don't leave me with that man, mum, mummy, please!' I was pleading now, frantic, tears rolling down my face and grabbing at her coat. I'd dropped to my knees, and the whole street could see us if they were in any way interested. She stepped back inside because my mother didn't like the scene.

'Don't leave me with that man.' I said, pointing at Charlie.

My mother cancelled her interview wearily and then sent me back off to bed with two more of those Ponstans for a lie-down. I know she called my grandmother and told her what I'd said, complaining that I'd cost her the chance at a new career because later, my grandmother asked to speak to me.

'Why did you do that?' She asked, which was a reasonable question.

I was sitting on the sofa downstairs with the phone to my ear, and my mother was standing over me with those small, brown, intense eyes glaring holes through the back of my skull, which was the way any of my telephone conversations went down.

'I don't know, Mama,' I said softly, 'I'm sorry.'

'You should thank your lucky stars for a mother like that and how she puts up with you, I'll never know. I never had this much trouble with either of mine. Wouldn't have stood for it.'

'But Mama,' as my mother glared down at me with one of her looks. 'What? What is it? You know you can tell me anything.'

'Nothing, nothing, Mama,' and then I handed the phone back to my mother, who grasped at it quickly.

'Do you see now? Do you see what she's like?' She was looking on at me with that playful smirk now, my mother, she was like a cat with a mouse. 'Do you see what we're dealing with?' I slunk off back upstairs while they agreed that I was just out to cause trouble again. After all Joan was always saying that Cathy was an excellent mother and an example to us all.

I noticed, though, that Charlie was quiet for a while afterwards, brooding for days. Thoughtful, in fact. They said, the grandmother and my mother, that the stress that I was putting them under had worsened his condition. Whatever the reason, he never came limping and lurching into my room again late at night when my mother was sleeping, reaching beneath the duvet, his thin, cold flesh crawling over my skin, and for that, I was grateful. But my mother discredited me and my character so effectively that it would not have mattered what he did because no one would have believed a word I said anyway.

When I disclosed some of this story to the therapist that day in her small cosy room, with my neat little handbag all balanced on my knee, I was an adult carrying around the various childhood versions of myself and all of their associated emotional baggage, stacked like a set of Russian dolls.

'I believe you.' She responded, calmly and sincerely across the room, like she was speaking in good faith and not because it was just her job to say that sort of thing. Well, I just cried for the longest time, apologising repeatedly for the eruption of tears because they would not stop pouring down my cheeks.

XXI

FACILIS DESCENSUS AVERNO

(The descent to Hell is easy)

My grandmother had a sister a few years older than she was. Fair like her mother and always smiling. Different from my grandmother in every way, who had always been dark. Dark and unsmiling. They say that my grandmother took after her father for that, but I could never tell from the old style of black and white photographs, which is all that remains of the man now.

From what I gather, though, this dark, distant figure overindulged his younger daughter, maybe knowing she would be the last. After all, war or no war, the family business did well enough. That's what she was, you see, a war baby, a child born in the first few days of the Second World War to the local undertaker: an ominous start for an ominous woman, and I often wonder how these international hostilities impacted her own more personal conflicts.

MEA CULPA

This second aggression came within living memory for those who survived the trenches of the Somme and remained numb from the shock of such an inhuman experience. Her father, of course, was one of these men. A soldier turned civilian who drank every night to drown out his own conflicted mind. The images of his young comrades screaming in the mud and the blood, begging for the sweet release of death. And when the pubs and the clubs finally closed their doors, he flung what was left of his ill-gotten gains to the wind for the workers to scrabble over in the first morning light. My great-grandfather was too old for the second war, but he never stopped fighting the first.

Anyway, she was a runaway, my grandmother, a runaway like me. She never talked of it much, but I knew. In fact, if she ever talked about those teenage years at all, it was always with distaste. She argued ceaselessly with her mother, by all accounts, and tolerated school for the purpose of only one lesson, which was an art class delivered by Miss. Quine, a teacher in her later years, never married and in the profession as a way of funding her own lifelong love.

These classes took place in the lofty heights of the upper rooms in the prestigious Rotherham Girl's High School building, looking over Clifton Park and its inspirational gardens. Here, my grandmother sketched and smudged, drew and painted, stuck and clipped, and learned to appreciate the masters, all under the careful guidance and encouragement of a kindred spirit.

When she wanted to leave school at fifteen, her father would not hear of it. He was a man of his time and considered this education vital for securing a reasonable marriage in the coming years. But my grandmother finally rebelled against the discipline of her Edwardian parents, and early one morning, slipped out while her mother was visiting the older daughter, Maria, who was married now with a home of her own. They were not close like sisters could be or should be, otherwise Maria could have been the one to provide a port in that terrible storm. So, Joan caught a train from the station and made her way to Filey, where her aunt and uncle owned a small establishment that sold teas and cakes to the summer holidaymakers. It was a happy place, a place of sunshine and sandy beaches, a place of smiles and laughter.

I can see her there now, at the station I mean, the air thick and heavy with the smell of oil and iron, the dense perfume of industry, progress, advancement, commerce. She would have sat against a stone brick wall on wooden seats replaced later by moulded plastic. A teenage girl trying hard to appear older than her years, so as to avoid the station master's suspicions. Her dark curls brushed back, cotton dress all prim and neat. She would have carried her mother's best coat and a small cream suitcase, hastily packed.

Like all runaways, she probably hoped that her parents would suddenly appear, gushing with contrition. I know I did. But she was a brave one, my grandmother, bold. Proud too. Too proud to back down.

They used to tell me that I was like my grandmother; I was my grandmother's daughter. Meant as an insult, naturally. But it was never an insult to me. She had a fire in her heart, did Joan, and a spirit that I always admired. Even in the later years, when she was left broken and bereft, a small ember of this force burnt on. Some days, some good days, her eyes would twinkle slightly with the force of it, and the bitterness would ebb away like the flow of the tide. The sight would make me smile because I loved her so, and even more when that gregarious spirit shone through.

Needless to say, Joan did not remain in Filey, and I am sorry for that, but at least she saw the summer out before returning, which was more grace than I was permitted.

She loved me too, or once she did, my grandmother. As a young child, I was one of those types who adhered to the standards set by the ideals of their wider society: pretty, pigtailed, and proper is what I was, perfectly moulded to project the image of what a little girl should be like in 1980s Thatcherite Britain, and she liked to show me off. Just a few years later, though, I had become everything a young girl shouldn't be: plump, petulant, and peevish, an altogether unpleasant adolescent in almost every possible way, and I was no longer the apple of her eye.

My mother never let me forget this fall.

'You used to be such a lovely girl,' she'd tell me either wistfully or accusatory, depending on her feelings at the time, 'I don't know what happened to you.' Her disappointment was palpable: she had hoped for better but had been stuck with me instead.

This is how we lived for years, me, her and Charlie, all cramped together in that oppressive little house with the weight of discontent upon us, hating and spiting one another for it, but each unable to shake the others off for our own very individual reasons. My excuse was always age, and my mother's was always impropriety; she worried far too much about what other people thought. As for Charlie, well, I think that his health conditions and frame of mind limited his options, so he continued to accept Cathy's increasing tetchiness with what can only be described as an almost saint-like degree of self-restraint. Because when my mother started on someone, she held almost nothing back.

'Can you hear them? Well, can you hear them?' she'd question us, pacing around the kitchen.

'They're nutters, all of them, nutters next door. He's talking to himself again. Can you hear them? Can you hear the voices?' Me and Charlie would just sort of look at each other and try to slink away while the episode subsided because we never heard these other voices ourselves but to say that out loud would bring about a torrent of abuse.

'She needs a psychiatrist, you know, a psychiatrist or a psychologist, one of those things.' Charlie would sometimes confide in me, and I would agree, although, to be perfectly honest, I didn't fully understand what either of these concepts really meant.

This was how me and Charlie began to sometimes form our uneasy sort of alliance, based around the unspoken principle that there was safety in numbers. This partnership would, on occasion, take the form of a seemingly rational conversation about my mother's recent outburst or a plea from Charlie not to take it to heart when she kicked off again, like one day when he was sitting on my bed talking.

'You've got to understand that she's had a hard life.' He told me, and I nodded, confused and ill at ease for reasons that I couldn't quite understand.

'So, you can't keep winding her up.'

Later that day I was absentmindedly drawing his initials in some solidified fat that had been left in a frying pan on the side for a few days. We always had a couple of pans hanging around, a big one for chips that were rarely out of action and then a frying pan that would be reused for sausages or other bits of ratty meat.

'What are you doing to that fat?' She pounced on me, and my mother did as soon as she walked into the kitchen.

'Nothing, Mum, I'm just messing.' There was really nothing deliberate about my actions.

'You're trying to get Charles into trouble, aren't you?' It was a senseless accusation to my mind because it was just a pan of fat.

'What's she doing now?' Charlie called over as he hobbled into the kitchen, like I was always up to no good, graffitiing fat and whatnot.

'Trying to get you into trouble. I'm sick of this, and I'm sick of this jealousy and attention-seeking all the time.' Was my mother's response.

Even now, I remain mystified about why drawing in fat with a dirty utensil would be classified in this way, but of course, it triggered the inevitable meltdown and became another example in the portfolio of a bad kid.

My mother quickly detonated in my direction while Charlie sat scowling behind her in his role as a supportive stepdad. I tried to deny that there was malicious intent to my scrawling in the fat, but the situation was hopeless, so I darted for the back door, but she met me there to prevent the inevitable escape.

She was tough as old boots, my mother, and she used to fill that doorway with her width. What she lost in height, she gained in brutality, and she would contort her pale face into a red ball of rage and throw insults out of it while remaining fixedly in place as I clawed around her at the wood to break free. To my mother, I was always stupid and a liar, exactly like my father, worthless and no good. She would grab my arms and hold me there, kicking at my shins and hissing in my face about how despicable I was, sometimes letting go of the odd shove until, eventually, she ran out of steam, and that would be my opportunity to make a run for it. She never liked it to go on for too long in case the neighbours got the wrong end of the stick and thought she was a bad mother. Once I was out of the door and gone, then she would wearily explain to the grandmother and the aunt over the telephone about how I had physically assaulted her while I limped off on my bruised shins to find shelter for the day and night and as long after that as I possibly could.

Hours or days later, when I finally rolled up having outstayed welcomes elsewhere, she would have admonishments from the relatives primed and waiting, and there was little point in trying to correct the narrative.

'She was shouting in my face.' I would sometimes try.

'Yes, but she's your mother.' It was always my grandmother's retort because it served her own purposes to believe that mothers can do no wrong.

Despite being deeply frustrated by the injustice of these scenarios, I think that overall, I probably believed that, too. Deep down, I knew that I was just another bad kid and that any attempt at defence would be inherently misguided since, ultimately, I deserved the shouting and the screaming and the shoving and the punching and the kicking and should learn to respect my elders. So, the next time I would try harder to be more submissive. Bite my tongue.

Ultimately, though, there was a history of me running away, although ordinarily, I didn't get too far. Also, a long history of 'arguing', as my mother described it. But perhaps because I had been more compliant when younger, then traditionally, most of our 'arguments' were conducted in the home and only as I became older and bolder did these altercations begin to spill out into the public hemisphere.

There was a time when all she needed to do was give me a look, this intense focus of those small brown eyes which would leave the pit of my stomach in knots, knowing that she was displeased and that this displeasure would all froth out when we were in private. Maybe around the age of fourteen, though, this very same look triggered me to froth out instead, even when we were in public. Like I said, I became a very unpleasant sort of child.

One time, for instance, we had a disagreement in Mexborough, of all places, which is an even smaller town a few miles outside of Rotherham. My mother loved to shop and would happily travel miles around to pick up a few bargains, so Mexborough became a regular place to visit since they had a few market stalls and cut-price shops, as well as charity shops, which my mother liked to hit every week as the new stock came in. I sometimes used to wonder if the neighbours ever saw bag after bag entering our house and start to question between themselves just where it all went because I had no idea how she fit all that stuff in our tiny home every week.

There were occasions that I could easily grease out of these jaunts on the basis that my mother truly wanted little to do with me anyway. Sometimes, though, she would demand my attendance, claiming a need for 'Family time,' and there was literally nothing that I could do to get out of going because it meant that she needed me for some reason. To help carry the bags maybe, or because she was going to force me to ask for a discount in a charity shop and they were more likely to cave into a child, or sometimes just because it was an opportunity to assert her authority. I was going, and that was that.

This one time, though, we ended up having a massive fallout in the middle of the precinct, and I can't honestly remember what it was about after all this time. I know that I was sullen that day, just incredibly miserable. Charlie was on form too, in an extremely bad temper, telling my mother to 'get her fuckin' sorted' all the way around, and I was dreading going home, knowing that it would all kick off again.

So, when things started to get hostile between us, I just walked away. Simple as that.

You see, Charlie had developed mobility problems and limped slowly on a cane, which meant that all I needed to do to escape from him was move faster. In an enclosed area, he could easily overpower me, but outside, he stood no chance.

It was an idea that came to me suddenly when things started getting ugly in the precinct. They were telling me that I needed disciplining, which was code for shouting insults for an hour while I snivelled on the floor like a dog, and my mother threw in the occasional kick to make sure the message rang home. I didn't want to go back to this, so I decided very suddenly to walk away.

Charlie set out after me, of course, his face like thunder with his brow furrowed out and his mouth in a dead straight line while he hobbled up the street, but my mother was relatively complacent about the matter. Charles always demonstrated more paternal responsibility and emotion than my mother by this time and tended to be the one who suggested coming to find me when I ran away while my mother was for watching the soaps and hoping I turned up in a few days. One way or another.

"Leave her," I heard her advise him, "We'll enjoy ourselves better without her here." Which I think was probably true.

He was all puffed out anyway, and she had already turned her back as I shot up the main street, quickly casting a final glance behind in their direction.

From Mexborough, I made my way back to Rotherham and then to the local train station, which is a small place with only two platforms and a small office that back then sold tickets but now just handles complaints about them. I'd withdrawn every penny I had from the NatWest bank account in my name and then used this for a one-way ticket to Hull and a packet of crisps because I hadn't eaten that day, and my stomach was growling nervously.

The ticket master was a little dubious at the sight of me, but he allowed the transaction to take place, and maybe it was the resolve in my eye that convinced him because he asked no questions about my age or parental supervision.

I was fourteen years old with dark curls brushed back from my face, shabby jeans over big black boots, and my old blue coat that smelled a little in the rain. It was fascinating to watch the newly built pacers pull in and out with their bright yellow faces and the old diesel giants smoke by in blue-grey clouds. I was excited to climb on board.

For me, though, this was the longest journey of my life, and I wonder now if my grandmother felt the same way. We never did compare notes. Sat in the jostling afternoon carriage on a worn Fabric stuffed seat, watching the people coming and going, and wondering about their lives, I was half afraid and half hopeful. I'm betting that Joan was just quietly determined. She was never daunted by much, my grandmother.

Hull Station was immense and formidable when I arrived, with people rushing back and forth, and it only occurred to me when I was standing there searching the stonework with my eyes that I didn't have my aunt's telephone number or address. Back then, we didn't have smartphones to carry all the vital information of our lives around, and it was just me and a ten-pence piece and a phone box. After walking around the city for a while, I finally took the plunge and dialled my grandmother's number instead, seeing her as a potential confidant. Of all people, I thought that she would be the one to understand my situation.

'WHERE ARE YOU? YOUR MOTHER IS WORRIED SICK...' She started shouting immediately, so I just hung up the phone. But I felt guilty then, so I dialled a second time, and she was calmer.

"We're setting off now. Stay put. Forty-five minutes. Don't talk to strangers." There were tears when she arrived. It was a relief, I think. She brought a feeling of safety.

'Mama, you don't know what it's like. Can I please stay with you and Grandad?' I pleaded with them when we got in the car.

'You just need to try harder to get on with your Mum.' She was always on my mother's side.

'Please, Mama. I can't stand it.' I was so desperate.

'It's not as easy as that, we don't have anywhere for you to stay.'

'She hits me, Mama, she hits me.' This was the first time that I'd ever told anyone. 'Oh, now come on, I don't believe that for one minute.'

'They walk around naked, Mama, it's awful.' Trying a different tact because I knew deep down that no one would believe me.

'Now you're talking rubbish. There's no way that our Cathy would behave like that. We'll talk about this at home.'

My mother and Charlie were waiting when we got there though because my grandmother had phoned her when I made the call.

'Car. Now.' My mother was livid. But then, anger was always her default emotion. I once made her a chocolate cake and she was furious because I'd used the wrong oil. You couldn't please my mother.

'I want to stay here.'

'Car. NOW.' Just like that, the great escape was over. My grandmother attempted to mediate; I was grateful.

'Aren't you going to come in for a cup of tea? You've come all this way.' She said hopefully, but Charlie was still in the driver's seat revving the engine of his Austin Maestro, face set like thunder.

'There are daughters out there who adore their mothers, who want to go shopping with their mothers, who help their mothers around the house and buy them gifts. Some daughters love their mothers, and look what I get,' she was pointing towards me now, 'that thing. Swearing at me in the street, embarrassing me, making me look like a bad mother. What does she have to run away from? She's got the life of bloody Riley. It's me that should be running away, me,' my mother told her tale so mournfully you'd think that someone had just spat in her soup, 'me, I'm the one that should be running from her! You don't know what she's really like.'

'Oh, come on now, Cathy, aren't you glad that she's okay?' But my mother wasn't listening to anyone now except that same old self-pitying tune in her head.

'All she does is want, and you can't get blood out of a stone mother, can you? To think I've raised such a nasty, avaricious, ungrateful child as that.' She nearly spat the words right out at me as I stood there in the headlights, watching the sea mist roll around my legs and bring with it the stark realisation of my blunder. I should not have made the telephone call; Hull was a big city to be lost in.

'You love her though, don't you, Cathy? Why don't you tell your daughter that you love her?' She had her moments, my grandmother, where she tried hard to make things better between us.

'Love her? Love that? How could anyone love that?' And with that, she turned to me, 'I said, CAR. NOW.' So, I got into the back of Charlie's blue Maestro, and while my grandfather nudged his little gold Honda down the track, we moved slowly away along the gravel toward home.

My grandmother stood looking aghast with her arms by her sides, and I tried to give her a little smile of reassurance as she brought her hand up to wave a feeble goodbye. There was an odd sort of finality to the moment.

For the next few weeks, our home was intolerable, with my mother pitying herself for having been given such a life and such a daughter and Charles mad as hell for me putting her in this sullen sort of mood. He liked a playmate did, Charlie, and her despondency was no fun for him.

Of course, I felt guilty and ashamed, but mostly, this quiet sort of acceptance just fell upon me like a blanket of ice-cold snow and with the weight of it, I began to comprehend life in a different way, a bleaker, darker, sort of way. Every day became a feat of hefty endurance with no promise of saviour or safety, no future to aspire towards or past reveries to reminisce over.

Although I could remember Old Lizzie-Anne and her soft curls and old ways, the feeling of fuzzy warmth was gone from the image of us sitting and playing our slow, unhurried games. There was nothing now but the desensitised daily struggle for survival: to eat, to sleep, to undergo the so-called 'Discipline,' and to force me through the motions of living such a life.

Alive but not alive is where I was. Caught somewhere in the middle. And this is when it came to me, creeping slowly into my mind and burrowing like a worm in dry earth. There could be a way out, a real way out for all of us. Like an old, broken vinyl, scratching away on repeat, came this black and cracked, worn-out sort of hope where no hope had existed before. An idea wrought of the ideas that flitted around our dysphoric little home at that time, fluttering around the melancholic walls and sad tear-stained rooms, because the idea of a way out was communicated so openly and freely in an open and free sort of language.

Charlie discussed it frequently, his way out, you see. If he didn't want to live anymore with these mobility problems, then there was always a way out. We talked about his way out, me and him, in the car sometimes when we waited for my mother to do her discount shopping. And my mother she talked about ways out, too, when it was just me and her sitting at the table over the spoils of those trips. How she should have taken a way out already if she'd had a mind. Maybe tonight she would do it. Maybe that night would be the night of her way out. Like her friend when she was younger. Oh, how they'd mourned when he got out. She admired him for it.

The dialogue of suicide was quite commonplace in our household, and it seemed quite a natural thing to do for a depressed, frightened, unpleasant teenage girl like me, unable to consider a future or life beyond this un-life. Why not just take the way out, I thought? Because the descent to Hell is as easy as that.

So, one afternoon, when my mother and Charlie were out shopping again, I rifled through her large medicine basket for something noxious enough to do the trick. Now, Cathy was one for hoarding prescription medication. When I had the psychiatric team in to help her out a few years ago, they were dismayed to find crates and crates of assorted pills all prescribed to various people, most of whom I had never heard of. She'd started the collection when I was a kid and just carried on for decades.

That day back then, on the way to Hell, I selected two bottles with difficult-to-pronounce names and assumed that these would be sufficient to do the trick. They were always talking about taking bottles of pills, my mother and Charlie. A bottle of pills would be their way out.

When my mother returned and set into me about something, I took the opportunity to drag the small MDF chests into place behind my bedroom door to ensure that there would be no disturbances. Nothing should interrupt my way out.

I knew that my mother was unlikely to check on me because, much like staying away for a couple of days, it was very commonplace in our household for me to be barricaded in my bedroom, so it would never occur to her to consider my wellbeing in there, in the same way, that she would not consider phoning the police when I had run again. Also, since my being voluntarily and involuntarily incarcerated was such a frequent occurrence, I had a few provisions hidden in the room, which was useful on this occasion.

I remember swallowing each tablet carefully with the contents of a flat and warm two-litre bottle of cola. The liquid was disgusting and syrupy but needs must.

Once the tablets were down, then I sat back and cried. It was the sudden feeling of alarm, I think that brought about these tears. But then, of course, I was always crying, so if someone outside the room heard me cry that night, they wouldn't have thought much about it. Other than, 'Oh, there she goes, fuckin' crying again.'

I sat with my ass jammed against the small chests and my feet wedged against the wardrobe, crying, which is pretty much how I lived three years of my life. It was a convenient location because my mother could still force the door open with her weight if she really wanted a good go at me, but not if I maintained this human wedge.

It seemed right to cry, and there was some solace to it. After all, why not cry? This was my way out, and if I wanted to cry now, then I could cry.

I didn't cry for the loss. There was no loss. But I cried when I considered what would happen when they found me, not me, but what was left of me, my body. The stinking, rotten, worthless corpse that had housed what might be defined as me.

I cried, thinking that she would be angry too. I cried because I was afraid. It calmed me, though, to think that I would be out by then by the time she found me. Also, because I understood on some level that the discovery would please her, so the anger would only be momentary and down to the disruption of it all. There would be some cold comfort for my mother in knowing that the opportunity could be utilised to her advantage. She would cry, too, and people would offer their condolences as her tears rolled away. I imagined that she might fan out my hair like she had in the hospital while people were watching. That she might hold onto my arm as they carried me away. There would be some sign of affection at long last. She did not love me living, but she could love me dead.

Sleepy then, serene, I crept to the bed under the window. It came over me in rocky waves the sleep, and then I no longer felt alarmed. In fact, the descent to hell was easy. There was no sudden urge to shout for help, to vomit the contents of my stomach, to halt the process of that ever-sleep. Let it come, let it take me, I thought. Let this be my way out.

XXII

INTER SPEM ET METUM

(Between Hope and Fear)

This was not to be my way out. I woke up groggy and sick the next afternoon, or possibly even sometime beyond this. It was difficult to determine how long I had laid there, sweating and stinking in my own mess, all tangled up in the child-like sheets with the big floral design that had been chosen for me, like everything else in the room.

Eventually, I stumbled out, climbing and scrabbling through the makeshift blockade to reach the bathroom next door. Almost immediately, though, I heard my mother jeering towards the television from downstairs, and oh, I cried then. Jesus, did I cry? I cried bucketsful.

Nobody had ever told me about this side of the coin, you see. That I might wake up. And in the days that followed, I was ill beyond measure. Indescribably ill. Just violently ill in my body and in my mind. An illness like you cannot imagine. Or maybe you can, and I am sorry for that.

My mother, seeing that I was unable to stand up straight for days or walk a line across the bedroom floor without holding the wall, the wardrobe, or the door to steady myself, well, of course, she made lurid accusations and instead of getting in medical assistance, wove some web about narcotics abuse on her daily telephone calls, which then became the new family narrative. It was another whip to beat me with, another example of my disgrace. The shit she had to deal with.

In all fairness, though, I never disagreed with her on the matter. To disagree would mean subjecting myself to more discipline, and I was world-weary and beaten by then, like canvas left out in the rain: sort of faded and unpliable. So, I hid the bottles in the dustbin before collection day and never spoke of the matter again.

What was there to say anyway? Even death didn't want me.

I guess it was around this time that I discovered a place that lies inside all of us, a void, if you like, a space that exists between the feelings of hope and the feelings of fear. It is an area arising from crushing nihility, where nothing can thrive but our own paralysis. Well, I crawled into that space, or perhaps what was left of my tortured psyche did, and I found comfort in the deadening stupefaction.

I dared not dream of tomorrow or reminisce for yesteryear. Instead, I remained numb, immobilised, frozen, and unfeeling. I was dead, but not yet dead, and so I lived without living for what seemed like the longest time. Days became weeks became months, and I can barely discern now between the events in my memory, any more than I could have discerned between the individual hours of any given day back then. Fourteen going on fifteen years old and blossoming into womanhood. Caught somewhere in a place between hope and fear.

What I can remember, though, is that whenever it was possible to do so, I would escape that wretched house with its wretched occupants and wander either alone or in the company of other teenage strays, who like myself, had been cast out by society and the worthless adults who they should have counted on most to keep them safe.

We were a displaced people, me and those I called my friends. Like all displaced people, we searched constantly for a home to call our own. Some nights, we would shield from the rain on market stalls that had been left empty by the retailers earlier in the day. Or now and again, we hid from disapproving glares under a damp bridge or leaking subway, but these sorts of locations could often draw unwanted attention, and we all knew that attention was a very bad thing. So, bus shelters, band stands, or the built-up seating area of the local bowling green were utilised in emergencies, but only as a last resort because they could often result in a visit from the officials in dark blue clothing who came to move us on lest our activity unsettle tax payers jealously guarding the market value of their cosy warm homes against hooligans like ourselves. Always, the prime location, if we could get it, would be an old crumbling building that had fallen into disuse. Here, we could claim some temporary foothold in the world, that is, until they came with their boards and their public orders. Never once were we asked why we huddled there like rats in the garbage because, to them, we were nothing more than vermin anyway, something to be eradicated.

Sometimes, my mother and Charlie would drive around looking for me, but other times, they didn't bother. Cathy had grown complacent about the problem of her errant child, and I usually rolled in sooner or later anyway to wash and leave again before the usual proceedings started. There were occasions when they stayed away themselves in an old static caravan that she had purchased for next to nothing, close to my grandparents' home in Hornsea. Although it was usually only a few days or a couple of weeks, their absence would be a wonderful time for me, and I would relax a little at home, clean the house up a bit, and try to make a good meal out of the scraps they left behind.

Of course, this respite would only make their return all the worse, with the shouting and the shoving and the accusations. Especially if I hadn't crept around quite mouse-like enough in their absence and the neighbours had happened to notice some sign of my existence, like lights or music playing. My mother detested intrusive questioning and would go up the wall if I'd given them a reason to consider her a bad parent. Like when my friend Nikki came around and we drank the cheap liquor from her mahogany reproduction cabinet, giggling together about boys we liked and dancing to the radio.

She was living with her foster family, Nikki, and I thought they were lovely. My mother used to tell me how bad I'd have it in care, but I'll admit to being a tad suspicious of this because Nikki said they hadn't hit her or anything. Still, she just couldn't settle. Too much disruption, I think, so we used to sit out, me and her, because we sort of had homes and we sort of didn't. It's a complicated situation to be in. We were like two alley cats left out to roam, and we never bothered asking one another questions when some mysterious new bruise arose or if one or the other had been missing in action for a couple of days. Some things are better left unsaid.

Anyway, it was Nikki who was there when I first found out about Poppy. We sat on a bench outside the local supermarket, watching shoppers give us dirty looks as they stepped past. Trash is what they were thinking. A couple of delinquents. Which is exactly how we felt about ourselves.

Nikki was good in a crisis, and she'd managed to lift a home testing kit as I made sure the store assistants were looking the other way. Neither of us ever had much more than a few pennies to rub together, and we saved what we could get our hands on for the bus. It was our getaway money.

Now that I think about it, there was some real cheek to going back in and using their customer toilet as well, but it wasn't something that I ever thought about at the time. Although it was something, my mother used to tell me often enough.

'Mum,' I'd ask, 'Can I have some change for the bus?'

'You've got some real cheek, girl, you have,' she'd chide, but sometimes she'd give me the money anyway to get rid of me for a day or two.

Anyway, the public toilet was grubby and smelled like a urinal. Not long afterwards, they fitted a blue strip light overhead to deter the junkies. There are moments when I wonder how many of those drug addicts had started out as the kids I used to know and hang about with. There but by the grace of god and all that. I thank my lucky stars in many ways for Poppy coming along, and I don't know where I'd be without her.

While we sat outside the old brick Tesco on Forge Island, though, I was flicking that white plastic stick about repeatedly saying, 'It must be wrong, it must be wrong. Please, God, not this.'

He'd told me that he just wanted to rest it there inside of me, 'Keep it warm,' he'd said. I couldn't get pregnant like that anyway; that's what he'd told me, and I believed him. Nikki rolled her eyes heavenwards when I told her this nonsense, but I wanted to believe him. It was somewhere safe to go in a world that was so inherently unsafe, and he let me sleep there in a bed with sheets and blankets whenever I wanted. Nobody screamed in my face or shoved and pulled me. No one kicked me in the back as I left the room, so that I fell forwards face-first onto the cold, hard kitchen tiles and hurt my lip. I was just so tired back then. It didn't matter that he was older than me, a lot older, because I was his girlfriend, and age didn't matter. I believed that bit, too. I told everyone we were getting married one day. I told them he was buying me a ring and everything. Nikki she used to look at me sort of sideways on and keep quiet, and I took this for jealousy. Always the fool.

My mother met him, and unlike Nikki, she thought that he was okay, which put us on better terms. Especially since I stayed there several nights a week and was out of her way, she never asked any questions, never spoke about what might be going on. We never talked about how he gave me chocolate sometimes afterwards, and I thought that I was living the dream. Or how he took me to the pub that time and bought me cider and crisps while he talked to a group of older men about me, and they asked if those were my real legs or if I was wearing tights. She didn't have a clue where I was, my mother, or what I was doing.

For me, the bubble burst the day that line turned blue, though, because that was when the fear crept back. It had always been there, really, just sort of waiting around on the sidelines for a way to get back in. I was terrified of what he'd say and terrified of what she'd say. Caught between a rock and a hard place with nowhere left to run.

So, after a while, I just started dodging. Staying home. Laying low. Focussing on the ever-expanding problem.

'How did your family not notice?' That was what my therapist once asked. A most excellent question because it was months before I finally blurted it out, and naturally, my mother was furious. Anger is always what she did best. He'd been on the phone pressuring me again, and after several months of this, she finally cottoned on to something being amiss.

'I want to know what the hell is going on!' She raged when I hung up. My mother had a nose for other people's distress and treated emotional anxiety like a rare delicacy. Of course, she dragged me directly to the doctor's office the very next morning, demanding an abortion be carried out pronto, saying I'd brought shame on the family.

When the physician performed an examination, she was peering obtrusively around the curtain because I was her property and had no rights toward privacy. Didn't he know that I was only fifteen and her responsibility? But that caused a bit of a shock because she had no idea how far along I was. There was an audible gasp when she saw the size of my stomach.

'Well, we had noticed what we thought was a little puppy fat.' She explained meekly to him afterwards with her handbag on her knee, giving me the deadeye sideways on.

This was nonsense, of course. I was stuck thin except from the stomach, and I think he said as much.

Anyway, the news launched my mother into a frenzy of activity, and in some ways, it launched my frozen mind from its reverie as well. I hadn't dared to dream or plan for a future beyond the next minute or hour, but my mother's reaction shocked me into the realisation that there would be a tomorrow, whether I was ready for it or not. So, I just joined on the bandwagon, and together, we collected and cleaned and collated baby equipment and merchandise from every nook and cranny, stocking our tiny house to the hilt with whatever might be required for a new and very small arrival. And my mother, well, she had a quite tangible and discernible shift in perspective towards me that was noticeable even in my highly anxious state. Nothing was too much trouble now, no task too arduous. At night, she would fan my hair on the pillow as I went to sleep, much like she did when I was young and in the hospital. During any medical appointments, she would stroke my arm reassuringly as the nurse performed her checks. Charlie, well, he just looked on, shocked and aghast, as the fanfare of tiny taffeta clothing and woollen mittens spread increasingly around him.

Despite all this fluffing and perfecting, though, I don't think that any of us really expected Poppy. Beautiful, bright, red, wriggling Poppy with her loud, demanding voice and tight little fingers that clung onto ours in her soft, commanding way.

During that long, painful, endless night, I remember the midwife bent down and asked: 'What are you hoping for, dear?' and I answered, in all seriousness, 'a set of new pans.' It was just all too much.

Of course, if you knew Poppy, then you would also know that she deserves more than to be a few lines in the final chapters. Poppy is a story all of her own. There are some people you see who are made up almost entirely of virtuous things, like honesty and integrity and dignity and righteousness. Poppy is one of these people. She can't help herself; she was just born this way. I should know because I was there. Right from the beginning.

There is an energy about Poppy, a sort of vibrancy or spirit in the way she steps in the fall of her honey-gold hair. When she smiles, if you watch closely, then you may note the effervescent twinkle of her eyes, like tiny tendrils of lightning are dancing through her iris. I wondered once if Poppy was really of this world or came to us, like some divine gift, a benefaction to thwart our perpetual misgivings. Because she brought with her something unheard of among us: laughter and sunshine, mirth and goodwill, she entranced us with her benevolence.

For hours, I would sit and hold Poppy. Looked down into her large, blue baby eyes that had not turned yet to their mature grey-green. I took comfort in stroking away the wisps of hay yellow fuzz that grew all fine like dander across her big pink head, and in return, she would look up at me and gurgle so that my heart would start to beat again inside. Tentatively, at first, unsteady and unsure of itself.

In Poppy, I knew happiness because happiness was Poppy. The smell of warm knitted blankets and tiny laced-up pram socks. Happiness was to love and be loved. It was the contentment of a baby's smile.

One time at my aunt's home, I sat on the floor with Poppy on my knees, sleeping soundly. 'It's okay to put her down, you know.' My aunt assured me, smiling.

'No, no. It's okay. She's comfortable.' How could I ever give up something so precious, even for a moment? But my mother, she scowled unhappily. It had been her turn to hold the baby. She wanted to play at dress up.

So, of course, Cathy, being as Cathy was, found a way to ruin it for us all. She planned, and she plotted, and maybe she had been planning and plotting from the beginning. But me, being ignorant and foolish, just as she'd always said I was, well, I just walked straight into her scheming hands. I did nothing to stop it from happening.

'This could be my second chance,' she implored. 'Don't you see? Don't you see what your life will be like? Do you want my life? Do you want to be stuck in a council flat with a baby? That's no life. What life is it for her?

Living on benefits. Have you thought about that? I'd be doing you a favour.' On and on she went. Jabbing away at my delight and targeting my already fragile self-esteem.

'You're not doing that right. Did you see her? Did you see how she moved the baby's leg?! She isn't doing it right. Give her here. You're going to hurt the baby!!!' She would glare at me while snatching Poppy away, wrenching off the Babygro that I had apparently fitted incorrectly.

Night and day, everything I did was wrong. Relatives who had come to meet Poppy would soon leave, uncomfortable by her incessant critique. The tension was palpable, and before long, my mother had taken over almost entirely. The crib was by her bedside, and the baby clothes were in her room. Only she could administer the bottles, and I was declared inept, unsuitable, and untrustworthy. 'No, don't come near her.' She'd snarl, and I heard her on the telephone complaining: 'She does nothing for her, nothing. She doesn't want her.' But I did want her, and I wanted her so very much.

Things came to a head late one night when Poppy was just a few months old. Charlie and I argued. He was complaining about my irresponsibility, and I was complaining about him walking around the house in only an adult incontinence pad with everything on display. The sight of it disgusted me.

I had been working part-time at a jeweller's shop in a local shopping centre, trying to make a bit of money to buy nice things for Poppy. This seemed like the right thing to do: going out to work. I wanted to do the right thing.

On the way home from a late shift, though, I'd left my bag on the bus, which was my first mistake. Then I asked Charlie for help, which was my second. He had given me a ride to the bus terminal but had been displeased at having to dress, and here was where the trouble had started. My mother became involved, of course, rushing to in his defence, and the shouting had reached a critical level, which was not good with the baby in the house. In the end, I just left through the back door. I couldn't take any more. How could I put Poppy through this?

The point is, though, that I went without Poppy. I left; Poppy stayed. I walked away. There was no way that I could have taken that little bundle out in the cold, hard night with me. She was too precious a thing to be risked.

In the days that followed, I went to the local housing office and tried to explain my situation, but I kept Poppy out of it. My mother had always told me not to mention the child, and she said people would call me a slag. When the housing officer telephoned her to confirm that I was homeless, she told him that this was not true and that I could go home at any time.

I think he understood the situation because he brought in a hot drink to explain all this, and we sat together for a while at a table over a box of Kleenex. All I remember is the apologies, over and over, apologising again and again for the procedures and rules that he had no choice but to follow. So, there we had it, over sixteen and not yet eighteen. I just cried small, choking tears, my life spiralling before me in a trajectory that I had never imagined possible. This is how it feels to be lost.

Once outside the building, panicking, I noticed a telephone box across the road. Charlie answered.

'It's okay. I'll come for you. Cathy, come here, she's crying.' Sometimes, I used to think Charlie genuinely cared for me somewhere in his twisted black heart.

'We think it's best that you don't come home.' This was all my mother had to say in the curt little voice she reserved for stomping out my aspirations.

'Mum, I've got no money and nowhere to go.'

'Yes, but if you tell them that at Crinoline House, then they will come and take Poppy away. Don't you understand that, you stupid girl? They will come and take the baby away, and you will never see her again. They will take her into care, and you know what they do to kids in care.'

She was earnest, insistent. I didn't really know what they did to kids in care, but I knew that losing Poppy was unthinkable.

'Can't I just come back home for a bit?' I hated myself for how I pleaded with her, but it was cold outside, and I was scared.

'No, you can't. This is my second chance. Don't you think you owe me that after everything you've put me through?' It was a low blow, but I knew that she was right. She'd had her work cut out with me. Everyone said so.

'So, what am I supposed to do, mother?' Imploring now.

'I don't know, but I'm sure you'll think of something.' I could hear the sneer in her voice as the line disconnected.

XXIII

MEA CULPA

(Admission of Guilt)

I never wanted to go back there, to that dark, dingy house, but the lure of Poppy was too great a draw. After a while, though, it became easier to stay away than to bear witness to her cheer. She was content, and that's the truth of it, beaming in her bright, easy chair, mashing away at the swirling plastic sea creatures in front, gurgling up towards us with her large, toothless grin. She found joy where I had only ever known desperation, and her jubilation became my despair. She didn't miss me at all, and why should she? Effervescent as she was, rejoicing in the light of her own illumination. And I felt fractured somehow to see her so animated amidst the debris of our former lives, to see my mother fawning, loving her as a mother should. Even so, I could not have put my hopes and dreams, my happiness, ahead of Poppy's welfare, not for a fleeting moment. She was my light, my life. And because of this, the lies came easily, landing softly like warm summer rain, settling delicate and reassuring in my overburdened mind.

'From now on, we'll tell everyone she's your sister.' My mother informed me. 'It happens all the time. Think about it, what life would either of you have?'

'But Mum?' I yielded so easily, placid like a sacrificial bull being led to slaughter. Eyes down.

'This is my second chance.' And she was luminous with it, my mother, glowing in the role of motherhood. Whereas me I was defective. Substandard in every way. What chance did Poppy have with a degenerate like me? Corrupt, debased, bestial.

'I'll get off then.'

'I think that's for the best,' my mother was laughing, enjoying her moment. 'You know what they say: don't call us, we'll call you!' She was skipping back and forth in front of Poppy, waving at me theatrically. 'So long, farewell, auf Wiedersehen, adieu!'

I was surplus to requirements.

Charlie looked my way, though, past the demonstration: 'I'll give you a lift.' I don't even know if she noticed him leaving. I guess he was surplus to requirements, too.

We sat in the car, me and Charlie, after this spectacle, sheltering from another chill November evening, waiting near the bus stop for my ride. A friend's mum had said that I could stay with them for a week or two. My circumstances were widely known. They'd all had a run-in with my mother at one point or another.

'What will you do?' We hadn't spoken in a while; we were both lost in our own thoughts. 'I don't know Charlie. I just don't know what to do.'

'I want you to know that I'm sorry.' He spoke gently, through lips barely moving, head facing directly to the front of the car.

'What for?' I wasn't sure if I wanted the answer. 'You know what for.'

'I don't, Charlie, I don't know what you mean.' 'I'm sorry for what I did.'

'I don't know what you mean, Charlie. I've got to go.' 'Your bus isn't here yet…'

I was already out of the car and fleeing into the darkness. After all, fleeing is what I do best. It wasn't too long after that night when we lost Charlie, though, his neurological condition having worsened over time. I wondered afterward if he knew his time was up. The stress of it had killed him, and they said, the stress of bringing up a problem child like me, that is. My mother agreed with them and mourned his passing like it were a Greek funeral.

Sixteen years later, she was still at it. Playing that same old tune and holding all the cards. Cathy, the poor widow. Cathy, who had been left holding the baby. Cathy, pulling all our strings.

Until one shrill November night, anyway, a night spent beneath cold Jupiter where I knelt choking, huddled, and trying hard to breathe through the asphyxiating blanket of fear. My own culpability hung like a figurative guillotine because I had left Poppy there, there with my mother, there with old Cathy and her voices. They're in a world beyond worlds, a dystopian nightmare made suddenly and alarmingly real again by the surges of eerie recollection invading my well-ordered life.

Furthermore, I remained powerless, entirely paralysed by my own intoxicating relationship with the fear, any resolve I managed to muster snapping like dry twigs under the manic tyranny of my mother's fury and manipulations.

Until now anyway, because like an old vinyl record worn low by the ravages of time, so too does history repeat the same cracked and distorted track over and over again.

This is my admission of guilt.